QUEERING
THE BORDER
ESSAYS

QUEERING
THE BORDER
ESSAYS

EMMA PÉREZ

 Arte Público Press
Houston, Texas

Queering the Border: Essays is published in part with support from the National Endowment for the Arts and the Alice Kleberg Reynolds Foundation. We are grateful for their support.

Early versions of some articles included in this collection were published in *Aztlán: A Journal of Chicano Studies, National Women's Studies Association Journal, Frontiers: A Journal of Women's Studies,* Indiana University Press, University of Texas Press, Third Woman Press, *Fifth Wednesday Journal* and *Edible Baja Arizona.*

Recovering the past, creating the future

Arte Público Press
University of Houston
4902 Gulf Fwy, Bldg 19, Rm 100
Houston, Texas 77204-2004

Cover design by Mora Des¡gn

Cover photograph by Adela C. Licona

Said s/he to the world

Working from shared perspectives on the body and its relationship to the natural world, Adela C. Licona scholar-activist-photographer photographs scholar-dancer Cara Hagan in the dried alkali lakebed of Summer Lake, OR. "Said S/he to the World" is an image from the "Shedding Skin" series of photographs that use the lakebed context to explore environmental desiccation and human/terrestrial relations. Assuming there is always more to see, this collaboration searches for ways of experiencing the world through a visual expression of relational insepa-rability. "Shedding Skin" is a visual production of and for developed intimacies with the land un-dertaken to cultivate conditions and possibilities for rekindled kinships and sustainable cohabitations with the human and non-human world.

Cataloging-in-Publication (CIP) Data is available.

∞ The paper used in this publication meets the requirements of the American National Standard for Information Sciences—Permanence of Paper for Printed Library Materials, ANSI Z39.48-1984.

22 23 24   4 3 2 1

PARA LUZIA, TE ADORO M'IJA

Table of Contents

The Decolonial Imaginary Revisited

Preface

When Arte Público Press approached me about reprinting essays I'd published throughout my career as an historian and aspiring creative writer, I hesitated because the early articles seemed dated. I realized, however, that a book such as this provides a map of one's evolution. The selected works in this collection begin with recently published prose poems that expand upon my notion of "sitio y lengua," site and discourse, a concept I proposed in the essay, "Sexuality and Discourse: Notes from a Chicana Survivor," in 1991. It was no coincidence that the idea came to me as I sat at my kitchen table in Houston having just returned from completing graduate school in California. Back in Texas, I felt immersed in familiar sights, sounds, tastes and smells. I became acutely aware of how much the space had imprinted my writing and as a result these simple words in Spanish, "sitio y lengua," emerged as an interpretive tool. I'm pleased the term has been taken up and popularized even if I may not agree with everything I claimed in that early piece. Still, I do think "sitio y lengua" honors sites we inhabit within our communities and acknowledges methods of communication, whether through food, or music, or poetry, all of which can inspire us to create new language that illuminates our past and present.

After graduate school, I was fortunate to land a job on the US-Mexico border at the University of Texas, El Paso. Living on the border from 1990 to 2003 guided many of the essays in section two. It was there that I began to imagine the queering of space and the decoloniality of language, which for me meant asking, how can we uncover the lives of those deemed invisible and how do we decolonize our minds? Those of us trained in the 1970s and 1980s were already posing questions to rectify the erasure of our stories and the neglect of our voices. We became determined to fill gaps and silences. In the mid-90s when queer studies transpired and facilitated the "queering" of bodies and documents, I wrote "Queering the Borderlands" to make a plea for locating the silences and gaps in methods often not legitimated in the academy.

By 1990 when I was writing drafts of *The Decolonial Imaginary*, I hadn't read tracts on the decolonial as theory or practice, other than Franz Fanon and Gloria Anzaldúa. The current decolonial school of thought had not yet developed as it has in the twenty-first century. I had come across the term, decolonial, in an interview of postcolonial theorist Gayatri Spivak, who refers to herself as a decolonial scholar, making the argument that decoloniality is a process. I studied postcolonial theory the summer of 1993 at the School of Criticism and Theory, and I realized Chicanx colonial history was not at the stage of "post" colonial. Instead, Chicanx, Latinx and Indigenous populations in the US live inside an ongoing process of decolonization. This means eradicating the colonial socioeconomic conditions in which we have found ourselves since the colonization of the North American continent in the 16th and 19th centuries. For me, the process commences with freeing the mind from our colonialist, patriarchal mindset. I coined "decolonial imaginary" to scrutinize how we interpret the world and to argue that we must look inside ourselves to dismantle oppressive ways of being. I continue to think of the decolonial imaginary as a deconstructive, interpretive tool—not to be confused with the tangible outcome of the decolonial project, meaning land. It's important to note that for Indigenous nations, the process of decolonization is meant to restore land.

In the last essay under the title, "The Decolonial Imaginary Revisited," I attempt to move beyond the decolonial turn to emphasize once again the import of the imaginary to discuss something I refer to as "the will to feel." In the article, I turn to the possibility of personal and collective transformations if we are willing to recognize who we have become and who we are becoming because of and despite historical and psychic trauma. In other words, the dictum, "feel your feelings to get to the healing," articulates the will to feel beyond the flesh and into the psychic terrain that Anzaldúa had already been traversing.

I have been fortunate to belong to a cohort of scholars and writers who temper our writings with our voices, our experiences and our feelings. We proclaim a phenomenology of self, a perspective grounded in personal and collective experiences from geographic, virtual and psychic locations—all this and more have shaped this collection. I'm indebted to Arte Público Press for reprinting these reflections.

Emma Pérez
Tucson, Arizona
March 17, 2022

SITIO Y LENGUA
(Site and Discourse)

Nopales

I.

Here, eat this, I say. You eye suspiciously the desert yield, a candied barrel cactus fruit so unlike an apple or a peach but you eat devouring the meat, the seeds, the juicy flesh and wonder what else I will offer as you sit, watch, judge and build more borders with elusive boundaries that will mean nothing to us, the ones who traverse spatial temporal fences across deserts while nourished with a fruit you never saw until we pointed to the desert floor. Lurking in a corner, I offer more. Only through the offering will I discover all that you are and not what you claim to be. You are a stranger, still the foreigner after centuries, after lifetimes never having seen or sensed or believed that an eagle, a snake and a cactus could create a myth so fervent that your antecedents, who condemned us, could not have predicted our thick-skinned persistence. We cannot be expunged. Or forgotten. We flourish. Even in the desert heat the saguaros bloom, the prickly pear ripens, birds sing and we thrive. We wait. We thrive. From this corner, hidden but not unseen, I see you laugh. I watch your greedy laughter as you pat your dogs lapping at your legs costumed in army green, a putrid green, not a life-giving green. And so you hunger for the fruit's palpable flesh as you mock me sitting patiently in the shadows studying others who try to inhabit you as I have tried so many years. It's a gamble. This waiting. This impetuous patience. Last night my companion in the desert asked, will our journey ever end? Will we escape? Of course, I lie. Can't you see? In the distance? We're close. So close to the end. I lie believing my convictions. I peep from corners where you won't suspect I might be. I take sustenance from the desert, a space in which borders and boundaries and *fronteras* are merely metaphoric lynchpins no longer geographic margins we are forced to abide but instead freedom of space overtakes, overwhelms. Newness is born. Yet we know that really nothing is wholly new. Maybe we seek an old way of being with holy forms of consciousness—*una frontera nueva* in which identities are supple and sacred to the touch. Like ancient seeds newly planted, reviving what lay dormant.

II.

What if you surrendered? Gave up and gave in to that which you've always known. An ancient knowledge gestures toward surrender. A spirit summons you to pause and look and see what you've refused to see. No one is asking you to sacrifice whatever. No one has said, there's only one way to love. You've narrowed your vision, you see. Look beyond the cracks and fissures to interstitial dreams and desiring bodies. Truth is not truth, freedom is imagined, the soul is transient, migratory, eager to go, ready to move across space, non-temporal, non-linear. In these dreams, time is unsettled, undone. Time is not time, space is not space, a heart is not a heart but an organ to play, to fine-tune and play like a magnificent instrument that screams and groans from being squeezed relentlessly through the evening's blue, blue night.

III.

Here, eat this, you say. My tongue grazes tender pulp. I take sustenance from ancient seeds—these kernels will expand into re-imagined landscapes. Of belonging.

Cages

Hundreds, thousands lost. No trace, they say. And yet there's the child on camera, in photos, terrified in cages or strewn across filthy floors with foil wrap as shelter. We need artists, creators of other worlds and dreams. We need painters, who render angels not forlorn, to draw spindly, fluid lines with pens in colored ink. Blue hues and red tints fused to stain an eagle in flames, or an orange phoenix resurrected from fire. Please, sketch the tender arms of a child no more than three, perhaps younger, perhaps older. Follow arcs and bends of prized brown skin and with skillful hand outline expansive wings like those of enchanted angels, angels with eyes melancholic. Hopeful. After the wings, take a razor, a blade and cut evenly, delicately. Carve ancestral names from clavicle to chest. Blood will ooze, trickle like ruby beads daubing tan skin forever marked to identify the unidentifiable. Inscribed like tattoos on bodies fragile and strong; promises whispered and broken. So much is broken. Transmigrating souls called infestations have been kidnapped and caged. There is tenderness here. That which we can't see, we must learn to love most. We must learn to love like that. Ethereal, like a cloud overhead we'll never touch or hold; we won't cry in those celestial arms. We've entered another panorama willing to learn a different, noble love. Not a love that traps, confines and dies from suffocation, no not that. Love is never caged or gripped or captured. Love is not a cage with brown children. This is an emergency. With pencils, pens, paints, blades engrave smoothly, precisely to alert, to warn, to identify the lost, which are not lost, but held captive. Name them. Return them from the unholy hell now embedded in their flesh's memory. As for the rest of us? To not forget, we invite you to brand us. With precision adorn our skin. With truth's accuracy lacerate surfaces, decoratively, deeply and engrave upon our flesh doves, peace doves, flying to their freedom.

An Epistolary Love Poem
to Sor Juanx

Querida Juana, Juanilla, Sor Juana, Sor Juanx,

I whisper inaudibly. I breathe into that place where your name resides, having taken refuge in my body. My epistolary expedition into desiring flesh. I begin whispering your name, and another's name, her name. How many Juanas in the world? Thousands? Millions? How many have been named to revere you, the muse of the new world, that terrain of conquest where inverse desires collide. Your own yearning, quelled and expanded into verse, and in that verse we feel every illusory nibble of flesh. Or did you deny the very thing in front of you? Because I have. And I do. And live to regret. Escaping to silences sometimes seems the only escape. And a nunnery? Really, Sor Juanx?

The carnal that is refused, run from, subdued, what's the good in that? Is it good we seek? I beg to be alone, to be on my own with my books. I know you understand. Over four thousand volumes in your library and you hungered for more. Books are the only constants; here we measure certainty with their comfort. Maybe we're both lovers of tomes and unpublished manuscripts, of unfinished love and lovers, transitory and impermanent. Isn't that all we want, Juana? To consume breath with the mouth of another. Of *the* other lover passing through.

Who is that woman asking you to be who you cannot be? In turn, you invite the impossible, but she is who she is and says she can't. Or won't. Instead, she tests. You are the test. A familiar experiment; you've been here before. She rejects suffocating regulations, repudiates the mundane that smothers, forbids, confines and proposes routine boredom, dull and average. The celestial body denying ingress. I mean, who wants to feel trapped, Juanilla? You with your trappings of faith, a faith that served your purpose. To live inside the walls of a nunnery, a bounty. So many women, you must have enjoyed the sublime irony. How many women wanted to strip in front of you? To delight in your gaze, seeking your stare, piercing and undeniable? They waited, didn't they? Would you extend a hand to graze the unadorned flesh of the other? You with your scathing passions, touching ever so lightly with fingers steady and willing. You tender a covetous look, a welcomed ploy in your domain, plunging reckless into illusive love, knowing she too will leave. You open the door, incite her departure and greet your freedom. A freedom as illusive as love. Passing moments with fictional lovers will do instead. We will resort to words on a page to feed the yearning and immortalize a name, your name, Juana. No one prays to be ordinary. Or predictable. To refuse that which is in front of you is a sin, don't you think? You chose not to sin, didn't you? And in that choice, you petitioned longing. But only on the page, Sor Juana? The safety of the page. Like a stranger's body, blank, then carved with shallow impressions.

"You don't know what you want," I said to her, and she responded, "I know I don't want this." And she sighed. Or maybe I sighed. Or maybe we sighed together. In unison we exhaled sorrow and uncertainty, accepting that which is outwardly real but not true. Only imagined. An interior imaginary recreates another truth. We make it up as we go along. Newness isn't always quantifiable, Juana. You savored passion and rebuffed the bigoted kinsmen, the priests and bishops who sought not to understand you, but to tame you because you were not who they wanted you to be. They sought to domesticate an inexhaustible mind and body, believing your soul was inferior to all things masculine, forbidding your masculine touch, fierce and tender in its willfulness, seductive in its cool resolve.

Perhaps they envied you. So many muses in and out of your domain, and the muse of the moment, satisfied and satisfying. And you, you wanted the way you wanted, when you wanted, how you wanted, asking for nothing other than divine pleasure. Some say authentic love does not ask, expect or plan. Today, we love. Today we take, absorb, integrate that which is ephemeral, yet infinite, transcending the mundane. See, there it is again, this need to live beyond the ordinary, beyond the past that imprints our present.

My body can't escape the marks, the bruises buried, secret wounds undetected except by someone like you, Juana. You who brandished a blade to cut skin and bleeding signed your name. You who refused conventional calling and lived in solitude, with conjured pleasures gracing your flesh each night. Did you dream of supple bodies, your face smoothed into skin so soft you melted from the scent you sucked in? Does it matter, now you hold instead a figment? A ghost? Or many ghosts, each visiting on an arid night to engage you in the games you loved. A corporal chess, strategically traversing a sweet terrain of slippery ardor, the power plays with no intent to win. Winning had no purpose. It was the game you coveted. Now that it's over, you gaze past vacant nights into milky skies where the ether holds all you'll ever need to know, Sor Juana—that time and space are arbitrary. Seasoned and sober, you compose passages in your mind, resorting to a blood-drenched finger mapping verses on another's flesh, her flesh. A memory inscribed with blood. *(She's there with you now, isn't she?)*

I wonder, did you get your kink on, Sor Juanx? On austere nights, did you grip a flogger or paddle and slap inside your thigh, imagining her or someone like her? Self-flagellation has its perks but is a lonely gesture for a well-versed lover. And penance? No, Juana, repentance is for fools, don't you agree? Tendencies unfamiliar to the common taste are still judged harshly. Come with me now and we'll visit carnal dungeons and stations of the cross where women dance and writhe and stretch pliant arms and legs taut against a wooden scaffold, keen to play candid games. A harmony of give and take so heavenly that corporal wisdom burns, adorning the skin with stripes of crimson and violet. And suddenly, this clarity, this peace. They will crave your attentive glances or a caress to prove your presence. Is it really you, so masterful at this sport, Sor Juanx? Will you surrender willingly? May I tie your wrists and ankles to a steel crosspiece and with pointed lashes wake your spirit? Your world illuminated. You, who have walked on ledges, escalating senses, rousing to dig deeper and deeper: did this outing, this spectacle of crosses show you others who desire like you? Who dig as deep? Yet you remain the dreamer in an empty cell. When you wrote of pyramids and Greeks and stars and eagles and a woman's touch, you hungered for affinity, a kinship no one shared. No one tried. But we understand. And we recognize how you requisitioned passion and summoned us to test love. To be something other than what was expected. Your passion, censured but not contained, lingers here among us, unveiling our dreams, these aching, infinite dreams. Sor Juana, we implore you to watch over us, the lovers, who burn and thirst and sweat through the night and wake to dream again.

Siempre,
Emma Pérez

Letter to Gloria Anzaldúa

January 2020

Gloria querida,

Amiga mía, te extraño. I've wanted to write to you, hoping you might hear me, not knowing if you can, but sensing you might. Something in the ether, invisible and daring, leads me to believe you are aware of the recalcitrant lies that overwhelm us. I often think you staged your passing to another dimension at a time when you suspected we'd need your spirit hovering, overseeing the hell so many Brown people are living. Do you send us messages from the other side, or is it me anticipating signs from you that will lead us to some redemption? Was it you, *querida*, signaling, when Carl Jung's book on dreams fell from a shelf and landed at my feet at the precise second I thought about something you'd once said to me? Some things are better left unexplained, you said. You, Gloria, were one of the first of our kind to try to explain who we were as Brown *jotería*. The 1970s were not kind. So many outbursts were necessary, so much critique to develop, so many histories inherited that had to be confronted to make room for new horizons. And so you gave us, some of us, many of us, words to survive by—something to assuage the pain of centuries, the wounds and blood of barbed wire borders meant to divide what was already fragmented. Your challenge: piece yourselves back together, *gente*. It's our only hope.

Could you have predicted how far this country would sink into an abyss of confusion, massacres and visceral hatred? You and I grew up in Tejas—Anglo, racist, homophobic, sexist, ableist, transphobic, classist, normative Texas—the "republic" that mirrored the rest of the United States. We knew well the primal loathing against all Brown people. We've entered the twenty-first century and find once again that ruthless aversions and phobic transmissions provoke the methods by which our communities think, feel and theorize this moment. White supremacy has invoked binary thinking again. Binaries, opposites, it's-this-or-that, it's-one-or-the-other—they have a purpose, I'm not denying. So do complexities. You attempted to clarify for us the complexities and gave us "Nepantla" to contemplate, study and reflect upon. At the end of the twentieth century, many of us wanted definitive answers; many of us wanted to point to enemies and say, you're wrong, we're right. We live in between spaces of longings; nothing is definitive. Not even death. I'm convinced you're reading this now, Gloria. Even in death. We all want THE answer. It's this, not that. We're all addicts seeking the one word that is THE truth. Not many truths but one truth. We're all addicted to being right.

Sometimes it feels as if we're trapped in cages like animals that eat each other to survive. Wait a minute: Brown people, Brown children, are trapped in cages—yes, real cages where they have been placed after being stolen from their families, from Brown mothers and fathers and siblings. And out here, those of us in privileged spaces, with various professions and occupations, are alarmed at how Brown continues to be invisible in this landscape of terror.

Not everyone will love us, or understand us, or care for the way in which we conceptualize the world around us. Not everyone will comprehend what it meant to grow up dirt poor on dirt floors with gringos outside your home policing your every move. Class privilege could not protect you. Heteronormativity and gendered cis-privileges could not protect you. Ableism could not protect you. With so many illnesses since childhood and no money for expert doctors to help a baby born bleeding, you struggled, often ailing, throughout your life.

I think about your current critics—not unlike those who raked you across hot coals after the publication of *Borderlands/La Frontera* in 1987. The critics went after the "straw men," so to speak, the easy stuff, the José Vasconcelos stuff, which is still haunting you. You said to me once, "I wish I'd known not to use Vasconcelos" in *Borderlands/La Frontera*. And then you explained that you had only wanted to publish the poetry in that book but your editors insisted you go home and write essays to elucidate the poetry. It was the mid-1980s, after all. Chicanismo was still obstinate in its "nationalist, patriarchal" tendencies. And so, you attempted to address the homophobia, the *"mestizaje"* that unfortunately rested upon Vasconcelos' racist, xenophobic theories (1925). You attempted to stretch that to consciousness, NOT biology, not phenotype. Instead, you built upon consciousness. You reassessed the term *"mestizaje"* in later works, perhaps in an effort to rectify the damage done by using a racist, anti-indigenous, xenophobe like Vasconcelos. You, like so many, had read him too quickly; and instead of seeing how he glorified all things white, Spanish and Western European, you too were somewhat enamored of a queer futurity that witnessed Brown in all its queerness, in all its transformation into a utopian space unknowable and seemingly impossible. Like José Esteban Muñoz, who wrote and published his first work a decade after yours, you too were trying to make sense of utopia for Brown. And like so many of us who didn't have a legitimated canon of theoreticians, or lengthy literature reviews, or historiographies, we built upon those who came before us, often tossing out what felt unusable. We were living at a time when a whole new feminist and queer and Brown era was starting to be conceptualized. There was so little that came before our own writings, and often what existed was intensely problematic.

You took to doing what Audre Lorde said to do; I mean, you were friends, after all, and you spoke often about how much you respected, admired and loved her. (You told me more than once and I envied that you had shared moments with her.) You disavowed the master's tools and devised innovative theories, sometimes using old Aztec myths. I remember arguing with "traditional" historians shortly after the publication of *Borderlands/La Frontera* because they attacked the book and deemed it historically inaccurate. I argued ardently that your concepts were conscious myth making. Based on problematic myths from a colonizing Aztec tribe, of course. You yourself knew that, but you refused to look to Europe, to Spain, to the Greeks, which I must admit I often do because I'm mesmerized by Oedipus, his plight, and Electra, her desires squashed. I'm Eurocentric that way, Gloria. And you knew it and you forgave me, my shortcomings expressed through my obsession with Freud, Lacan, Foucault and the French feminists. And all the while you besieged us to look south, to acknowledge the erasure of tribal groups in the south even if it meant we paid too much attention to Aztec lore. But conscious myth making is still myth, and although fables have purpose, that purpose is often outlived.

Do you want to know what annoys me most about some current critics? The binaries. The way in which some faultfinders have fallen into that trap of yes/no, black/white, man/woman, good/evil, of the binaries you attempted to dispel with complications, with consciousness about teeming differences, including queerness. I remember you told me you didn't particularly like using the word "lesbian" because you had nothing to do with that Greek island or with Sappho. Again, you wanted us to look south, not to Europe. It was a historical time when Europe and all things European imposed so much upon our learning, whether Marx, Engels, Althusser, Emma Goldman or the anarchists of Europe, who also influenced Mexican anarchists. There it was again. The north imposing upon the south. And you wanted to contest that over and over again, and you did. And yes, you made mistakes, as we all do when we have so little to draw from. We find ourselves creating words and concepts that should be revised and re-energized or simply dropped, the way you dumped Vasconcelos and his notions of mestizaje and focused upon "*nepantleras*," the in-betweeners—or, as the brilliant Lauren Berlant calls it, "the impasse," which is that state of being in between. I think you would have liked Berlant's *Cruel Optimism* (2011), Gloria. I think you would have liked Muñoz's *Cruising Utopia* (2009), and you would have known how to appreciate Juana María Rodríguez's *Sexual Futures, Queer Gestures* (2014) for the way in which Latina longings are detailed. I think you would have understood the intricacies that also theorized beyond binaries.

When you spoke about our community's "*jotería*"—saying openly what had not been said before: "listen to your *jotería*"—you took a chance. I remember you recounted for me the way in which you were treated at the National Association of Chicano Studies conference (before "Chicana" was inserted into the organization's name), held in Michigan in the late 1970s, and how the brutal homophobia cast you out of those conference rooms. You swore never to return. But you did finally when you saw that a group of Brown queers had intervened by the 1990s—more than a decade after you had been run out for being a Brown queer confronting the nationalist patriarchy of that moment. In 1990 you returned to the historic Albuquerque conference of the National Association of Chicana and Chicano Studies (NACCS), where a core group of Tejana "lesbians" fought hard for a lesbian caucus and the "*jotos*" organized their joto caucus. At that time, we felt a need for gendered, safe spaces. Many couldn't see the trans-phobia that was so damaging. I always regret that. We did attempt to remedy the trans-phobia in Miami by expanding the lesbian caucus to include bisexuals and transwomen/transmen.

It's somehow fitting that you were finally recognized as NACCS Scholar of the Year at that same conference. Posthumously, of course. *Después de atole*, as we say in Tejas, *¿qué no?* You would have approved of the inclusivity because at your core that is who you were.

I list all this to recount our many mistakes; hopefully new critics may learn from our past just as we learned. Or maybe not. Arrogance is so much a part of youth, I know. My own arrogance in your presence sometimes stemmed from my insecurities, but I think you know how much I respected you. I marveled at you, at your Tejana origins and how you'd persisted without the privilege of formal training. Self-taught in so many ways. I mean, you read Kierkegaard for answers to your growing "anxiety." You read Marx's *Capital*, you knew Derridean deconstruction, you understood Foucaultian discourses on power/knowledge: hell, you lived it.

At a recent NACCS conference, I heard reverence for your writings at the same time that I heard absolute disdain. I don't object to those who dismiss your theories and methods if the concepts do not resonate for them. Many of us reject that which doesn't feed the core of who we are. I don't even care about those who dismiss your work without reading it closely. What concerned me at the conference were the statements that implied something like this: "Someone's freedom can be another's chains." In reference to your work. Yes, I heard that. It made me angry at first and then I got sad. To argue that all your work be dismissed because it felt like "chains" to an up-and-coming population of critics? I can understand the criticism about your misuse of Vasconcelos' *mestizaje* and I can understand the necessity of that critique. But what about "critical mestizaje," to quote Rafael Pérez-Torres (2005)? Perhaps that is what will move us beyond the "hybrid fantasy" encompassed within a *"raza cósmica"* that privileges "whiteness" (Vasconcelos 1925). Weren't you leading us toward critical mestizaje all along when you asked us to consider the power of "consciousness?"

And what about your other concepts, Gloria? What about *autohistoria* as mixed genre for writing life stories, *desconocimiento* as willed ignorance, *la facultad* as intuitive knowledge and *el mundo zurdo* to highlight the often-neglected "left-hand" perspectives of women and queers of color? These are in themselves methods that expand upon a critical mestizaje, a tool to critique power and inherited histories of violence. And how about the way you revered "*la chicanita*" y "*la prieta*," the dark one, as you were called growing up? Will we be asked to toss out all your words? They still resonate for many of us.

Your work, your nonformal training, is criticized by those with class privileges, with PhDs from premier universities, with race/gender/heteronormative privileges—all these privileges that allow for intellectual critique and engagement—things you didn't have. You fought to stay alive with an illness that wore you down. With no steady income and dubious health insurance, you had to go on the lecture circuit, which wore you down and wore you out. Remember when you came to Santa Barbara for a couple of weeks? Chela (Sandoval) insistently drove you to many health food stores and herbalists and you complied because you knew she was acting out of love for you. She and I feared you'd leave us too soon. And you did. I guess you got tired, Gloria. Who can blame you? The little critics are still here and they are exhausting, let me tell you. They say you are anti-Indigenous and anti-Black. Again, the haunting of that dire mistake of using Vasconcelos. We need to hold ourselves responsible for our mistakes. You did. But I suppose some people need those straw men to feel their own sense of comfort in this craziness we're living during Trump times. What an evil idiot. I resent any and all who are anti-intellectual and don't conduct thorough research, but instead rely too much on blogs and populisms in social media, as do certain figures in the White House. I'm old-fashioned, clearly. I still believe in reading as much as possible, listening to as many opinions as possible and sometimes getting it wrong. And sometimes we make some progress despite existing on the margins of so much, including academe, including social networks, including community work, including Hollywood films, including New York's "big lit" writing elite. The critique of Jeanine Cummins's "big lit" novel *American Dirt* (2020) as purveying cheap sensation and stereotypes about Mexican experiences would amuse but not surprise you.

I ask, as you would, how do we talk to each other now? How do we respect each other? How do we learn from the past? I'm still a historian at my core. I can't help myself. Which reminds me, I saw on a blog someone criticizing your work because you didn't cite recent publications. They assumed *Borderlands/La Frontera* was published in 2006, which is the reprint date, and I suppose the assumption is that even after death you should have revised what was published in *Luz en lo Oscuro* (2015). It's all so messy.

I'll admit, however, that it's so refreshing to be with the writers in this dossier who confront some of the messiness of time, in time, addressing voices past and present that are crying to be heard. Here, we do what we know how to do: engage, listen, critique, write and hopefully learn something from listening to each other. Hopefully, hopefully we attempt to learn how newness, painful as it may be, must come into being.

But before the newness, we are in this specific now. Times are rough, *estimada* Gloria. Brown children are in cages. Brown *gente* are in detention centers. Brown people are hunted down, as are Native and Black people. Brown and Black queers, transwomen and transmen are hunted down. Yes, we still live with hierarchies that dehumanize people of color. And the white allies who speak up, well, we need them too—the ones who willingly stand in the line of fire.

Gloria, *querida amiga*, you died at the young age of sixty-one. The white, colonialist, heteronormative, cisgender world you inhabited took a toll on your body, your psyche, your mind. It wore you out. It wears us all out but some more than others. Some get even more ill as a result of genetic and historical trauma. But what we know today is that we're living a world that is currently dictated by fear and hate. If we turn to some of your methods, we can focus on their power and function that advised us to heal colonial wounds. You asked us to embrace the Coyolxauhqui imperative to piece ourselves back together as we orient our disoriented selves. You ordered us to become *nepantleras* weaving in and out of hegemonic spaces that do not acknowledge the beauty and grace of differences. *No sé*, Gloria, *querida mía*. Today, we're on the brink of yet another war that targets Brown and Black people; Indigenous women continue to be raped and murdered more than any other population of women; Puerto Rico has not recovered from its earthquakes and massive hurricane; Covid-19 is hitting Brown and Black people hard in many US communities. As I write this letter to you, people are in the streets protesting the murder of George Floyd. Police brutality mostly goes unpunished and is unending. Our anti-intellectual president has been impeached for his predatory lies, but so long as white wealthy elites champion him, there will be no consequences. What's the solution to all this desolation and greed? How do we search for the light in the dark, as you prescribed? A leap of faith is all I know anymore, *querida* Gloria, and I consistently remind students to err on the side of hope. I mean, why not engage an ambivalent hope, an awkward hope, a tricky hope, a hope that may open us to less fear and more love—a hope that buries colonial wounds so they never resurface. These are a few of the many things I learned from you, *querida*. These things and so much more, and for that *te doy las gracias*. I hope you're resting and I also hope you're overseeing this messiness we're living. Send us signs and signals, Gloria, if you can. Many of us are still listening.

Siempre,
Emma

Sexuality and Discourse: Notes from a Chicana Survivor

> "Don't remain with the psychoanalytic closure. Take a look, then cut through."
>
> —Helene Cixous

My socialist feminist bias has spurred me in this direction. When I was a budding graduate student in Chicana/o history and Women's history, I tried stubbornly to show that class-based movements subsumed gender.[1] While Chicano scholars argue that race must be integrated into a class-based revolution, many Chicana scholars defend that the secondary status given to women's issues in a race and class-based revolution cheats the revolution.[2] We are tired of debating the same questions that plagued Alexandra Kollontai in Russia to Hermila Galindo in Yucatán in 1917. The global socialist movements in the early twentieth century in Europe, Russia, China and the Americas inevitably found women forced to place gender issues as secondary to male-defined arguments. Ironclad men assumed they knew what was good for all workers. Women wrote and women spoke. But they were not heard.

I turn from the socialist feminist debate and assume that those of you reading this essay agree that the "unhappy marriage" between Marxism and feminism remains the chosen marriage given that the alternative for feminists is capitalism, a deadly, destructive "husband."[3] We opt for the man, who, as our mothers point out, "*Sí, toma, hijita, pero no te golpea*" (Yes, he drinks, but he doesn't batter you). He is far from perfection, but as socialist feminists we tenaciously hitch ourselves to the man we are desperate to change to improve the marriage. This "husband" has potential if he quit his ego-driven anxiety that defines his world on his terms. But, at least with him, there is the potential for equality and freedom. With the capitalist, we are battered, raped and left to die in the factories, fields, bedrooms and boardrooms. From the Marxist, we hear that "women are oppressed," as he gathers with his male cohorts, then yells to you, "Hey, honey, bring me another beer." Lip service is worth something, whether it's in the boardroom or the bedroom but it is not a revolution.[4]

I reassert beliefs that evolved in my young days as a radical feminist, that is that sexuality and our symbolic reading of sexuality is the core of the problem. The problem: before the revolution, political, Marxist men refuse to give up their power, during the revolution, men refuse to give up their power, after the revolution, men refuse to give up their power.[5] And what power do we mean? Social, political, economic and yes, sexual power.

In this essay, I want to take us beyond the antiquated Marxist-feminist debate, assuming we agree that class struggle is unavoidable and assuming we agree that race-gender analysis and sexual autonomy must be the vanguard of a victorious revolution.[6]

The question is, how are we going to achieve such a revolution given the strength and persistence of the patriarchy? I define my analysis of the patriarchy by invoking Freud, Lacan and Foucault, if only briefly. I take from the French feminists who deconstruct male-centered psychoanalysis—Helene Cixous, Marguerite Duras, Luce Irigaray, Julia Kristeva et al. I take from them what is useful to me, and I find their aphorisms often brilliant. Deconstructing white European feminism to reconstruct Chicana feminism may appear inorganic. It is as inorganic as taking from Marx, the quintessential white, middle-class, European man, to explain the exploitation of a Chicana in the cotton fields of Texas. Consciousness is born out of one's intimate awareness of one's oppression. Theoretical models can often provide short-cuts to dissect exploitation.[7] Just as Marx provided a paradigm to grasp the relationship between worker and capitalist, I claim that Luce Irigaray, particularly, and other French feminists offer a paradigm for me to interpret sociosexual relationships and hierarchical structures between and among heterosexuals, lesbians and gay men.[8]

But, where does culture, race and colonization fit into the paradigm? Neither Marx, Freud, Lacan or Irigaray explain colonization and its effects upon people of color. Hence, I am drawn to writings by women of color who deconstruct the male or European tradition that has usurped our power since Columbus landed in the Americas. Gayatri Spivak dissects colonization as she deconstructs the power-wielders, Jacques Derridá, et al. She takes issue with the French feminists, and for good reason. What I hope to do, however, is to highlight the significance of sexuality to observe how sexuality is expressed for colonized people, especially women. How do we, as women of color, integrate an analysis of sexism with racism to deconstruct their pervasive ideology? How do we liberate ourselves from the sexism in our Chicano community while we combat the insipid racism in Anglo society? How do we respond to sexism within colonization, given that men of color experience racial oppression and displace their frustration on to women of color? I cannot begin to answer all these questions, but I articulate them to acknowledge the complex problems we face as women of color. I turn back to French feminism to place the argument back upon sexuality, because sexuality remains an obscure controversy in our Chicana/o academic community.

I also turn to writings by radical women of color. Gloria Anzaldúa and the writers in the important document *This Bridge Called My Back* reaffirmed the organic movement that has been

alive in the women of color community since the 1960s.[9] Norma
Alarcon's Third Woman Press, Kitchen Table Press and Arte
Público Press's publications by Chicanas and Latinas, and other
journals that I have not named, are vital mediums for women of
color who publish work that is rejected by "mainstream" presses.
My Chicana *colegas de* MALCS know this dilemma only too
well. Chicana scholarship in mainstream feminist journals like
Signs and *Feminist Studies* is grossly underrepresented. As Chicanas, we face the same problems that white women face when
they attempt to publish in male-centralist journals. The arguments
that men pass down to white women are passed down to us. We
are forced to address issues as they define them, not as we define
them. And, of course, the issue of "academic standards" haunts
us. This essay does not address this publication problem directly,
nor will it deconstruct writings by women of color. Indeed, our
work reconstructs as much as it has always deconstructed the
white-male order and white-feminist assumptions about women
of color.

Ultimately, when women of color break the silence, our
words are rejected. I wish to point out that our works emerge
from *un sitio y una lengua* (a space and language) that rejects
colonial ideology and the by-products of colonialism and capitalist patriarchy—sexism, racism, homophobia, etc. The space
and language is rooted in both the words and silence of Third-
World-Identified-Third-World-Women who create a place apart
from white men and women and from men of color, if only for a
weekend now and again.[10]

The essay has three parts: (1) it will reevaluate the Oedipal
moment when men recognize they have sociosexual power, and
it will amusingly speculate on how Chicano males hold that
power ambivalently; (2) it will assess "the molestation memory,"
or "memory of origin," when girls recognize they do not have
sociosexual power in relation to men; (3) after moving from male
power to female powerlessness, the essay asserts female power—

how Chicanas seize sociosexual power that creates our own *sitio y lengua*. So I move from deconstructing male centralist theory about women to reconstructing and affirming a Chicana space and language in an antagonistic society.

As an historian trained in Western European tradition, I ardently question white male ideology and white women's assumptions about women of color. Hence, I deviate to the French feminists with a degree of ambivalence. Theirs is not my "language" and theirs is not my history, exemplified by conquest and colonization. Indeed, Europeans *acted* a history as conquerors and colonizers. French feminist discourse deconstructs white-male language, but the method also builds upon what they destroy, one of the pitfalls of deconstruction. They argue for women's method and culture, yet ignore racial memory. The French feminists, however, rebel against that which I, as a Chicana historical materialist, also resist—the male symbolic order. The way the French school dismembers male dominion is what intrigues me. By scrutinizing their offerings, I attempt to supplement an analysis for Chicanas that chiefly summons sexuality and embraces sexuality's relationship to race, class and gender within our culture.

Implicitly, the analysis questions choices we make about lovers based on race, or ethnicity, class and gender. Who do we choose to love and to have sex with, and how do we make those choices? I imagine that we each have fundamental, core issues that help us decide who to choose as our lovers. Those core issues can be traced to a precise historical moment, usually at childhood, when something occurs to push us in a particular direction.[11] Heterosexuals who choose to love heterosexually within their own race and class do so for what reasons? Because society constructed them as such or because they desire it? Or because they desire what society desired for them? Lesbians who love women within their race and class do not do so because they were socially constructed to love their own gender, or were they? Lesbians may have been constructed to reflect culture, but gender?

As I address sexuality, I also pose that pervasive homophobia constructs sociosexual power relations in society and pervasive homophobia in our Chicana/o community limits the potential for liberation and revolution. For most heterosexual Chicanos and Chicanas, internalized homophobia and bisexual ambivalence frightens them into a rigid analysis of our community and of the Chicana/o family.[12] Studies in the social sciences on the Chicana/o family which ignore the existence of alternative lifestyles and "women-without-men" only serve to perpetuate Anglo perceptions about our community.

Many Anglos, particularly white feminists, insist that the men of our culture created machismo and they conveniently forget that the men of their race make the rules. This leads to problematic Chicana discourse within feminist constructs. When white feminists ardently insist upon discussing machismo, they impose phallocratic discourse. By "centering" and "focusing" upon the penis, they deflect from their racism. This evasion is both racist and heterosexist.

After providing what I hope is simple criticism in simple terms, I despise mystified abstractions about the obvious, the oppression of women of color, I hope to offer simple solutions to daily antagonisms—faith and hope for our future embodied in our spoken words and in our writings.

"Men must cease to be theoretical imbeciles."
—Margarite Duras

To address sexuality, discourse and power, I digress briefly to male theoreticians who, I believe, best defined male behavior.[13] Freud, Lacan and Foucault classify male behavior, exalt it unknowingly, but where women are concerned, these men were and are "theoretical imbeciles."

Let me begin with Freud, the omnipotent father. The Oedipal moment is basic to his discourse. The moment occurs when a boy, the son, realizes he cannot have his first love object, his mother, because she belongs to his powerful father. He fears this man whose phallus looms larger than his. Inadequacy and fear ensue because "his" is smaller, but the son's fear swells when he realizes that his mother does not have one. Therefore he, like a woman, could dreadfully lack one, hence castration anxiety is linked to his dread of women. The son repudiates the mother and allies with the father because they both have a penis, but he still competes with this powerful father. He spends his life proving his is "bigger" and "more powerful" than any man's or than any symbolic father's.

But he also preoccupies his life with renouncing his mother at the same time that he searches for her. Hence, his Oedipal complex is never resolved, and in this fear and anxiety he acts out against women. As Luce Irigaray elucidates, "The little boy will never cease to desire his mother."[14] His acting out, so to speak, is found repeatedly in his making a society where the laws, ideas and customs permits him to reenact the Oedipus complex. All he has to do is give up his desire for one woman.

Thus the—fictional—disappearance of the Oedipus complex would resolve itself into the individual's ability to make capital out of ideals and (thereby also) out of mothers, wives-mothers, laws, gazes Oedipus will have all the mothers he wants, all laws in his favor, and the right to look at all, or most, mothers, laws, views (or at any rate points of view). Oedipus will be rich and have no complexes about it. All he has given up is the desire for a woman, for a woman's sex/organ because in any case that had no value (p. 82).

Irigaray links capital with the persistence of the Oedipal complex. Men must reify their desire for their mother in rules, laws and social constructs that deny women their existence. Pornography, a result of his "gaze," helps him swear that he no longer suffers from Oedipal anxiety. Women become his idea—castrated, passive and eternally feminine in his eyes, in his gaze. As long as he can "gaze," as long as his "love of looking is satisfied, his domination is secure."[15]

Lacan imparted to us the "symbolic law of the father" entrenched in language.[16] Language, he argues, is ensconced with symbols that dictate patriarchal power. But in his discussion he, like Freud, dismisses women, and exalts the phallus, again because women do not have "one."

The French feminists argue that Freud and Lacan place woman "outside the symbolic" . . . outside language, the law, culture and society because she "does not enjoy what orders masculinity—the castration complex."[17] To the French feminists, the patriarchy is a law of death, of destruction, of violence. Maleness is socially constructed to be competitive, maniacal and violent—all rooted in the castration complex and evident in war, violence against women and children, rape, battering, sexual molestation and nuclear weaponry shaped like penises that ejaculate death. The violent conquest of Third World people mastered. Femaleness, on the other hand, is socially constructed to be collective, intuitive, creative, life-affirming—the other.[18] But women who accept the symbolic law of the father perpetuate it and in essence become like men, women in drag.[19] They might as well be men because they defy bonding with women, allude that men are superior and therefore more worthy of their intimacy. Women, however, even when they accept the law of the father do not rape, batter and sexually molest children in the horrendous numbers that men do. Hence, it is the symbolic phallus, the tool of oppression, reified in their guns and bombs, that reduces men to dangerous imbeciles. Their death drive tested.

Foucault, finally. Foucault transcribes historical documents to ventilate "the power of discourse." He argues that "through discourse power-knowledge is realized."[20] Language, after all, is power. Third World people know that to learn the colonizer's language gives one access to power and privilege, albeit controlled, qualified power. As an historian, I explored Foucault because he scans the history of discourse on sexuality. I read *The History of Sexuality*, Volume I with curiosity, but soon discovered that Foucault, like Freud and Lacan, spoke to men, about men, and for men in male language.[21] In a single paragraph, Foucault "thrust," "penetrated," "rigidified" and "extended" power.[22] By the end of the page, I felt violated. Such imagery of "seminal" ideas "ejaculating" on paper made the reading painful at first and then comically apparent. Are these male theoreticians so pained with castration anxiety that they must spurt on paper at every given opportunity? It is precisely this kind of male writing and language that rapes, numbs and dismisses female experience at every stage.[23]

Because Foucault commits his study to the history of discourse, he restricts himself to male-defined arenas where women are both absent and silent. Surely, he knows that, but he does not seem concerned. When he argues that the discourse changes through the centuries, I am suspicious because he informs how men's language about sexuality and power has changed. But he doesn't say this. Like Freud and Lacan, he would like women to absorb patriarchal interpretations at the expense of sanity to reconfirm hysteria. As the other, the object and not the subject, women remain objectified in Foucault's discourse.

My impatience with Foucault, however, is in what he neglects to say *The History of Sexuality*.[24] While in the last chapter, he finally discusses power and its relationship to sexuality, he overlooks the obvious. Like male theoreticians who build abstractions to mask the simple, he does not say: men, especially European white men, hold political, social, racial and sexual power over women; and men use that power throughout history to control women and to sustain patriarchal power. *Punto.* Is this premise transhistorical? Is it cross-cultural? Yes and no. Every aberration of sexual abuse against women and children of all races and men of color has its historical antecedents.[25] This, I believe, is a point of departure for women historians.[26] For Chicana historians, we begin with what Foucault does not say.[27]

Why can't Foucault declare the obvious? Because he is blinded by his privilege, his maleness, or because he cannot chip away at his own power? Surely, it's not that simple. But I cannot spurn Foucault so easily. Again, as an historian, I appreciate his historical specificity, because within his constructs he forces me to ask if indeed patriarchal power is transhistorical. And, is the Oedipal complex transhistorical and transcultural? Is it useful to Chicanas writing history when sexuality is so inextricably enmeshed in our history of conquest and colonization? The question leads to the next section.

As an aside, I acknowledge that male theoreticians, whether Marxist, deconstructionists, or traditional social scientists, often dismiss feminists and our analysis as bias, especially if the analysis is from radical women of color. I invert that arrogance to dismiss most male perspectives about women because they are much too self-indulgent to comprehend our oppression—that intimate place where theory is born. Men of color understand their own tyranny just as white working-class men potentially understand their class exploitation, but many working-class men and men of color refuse to take that sensitivity to its logical conclusion where women are concerned. Working-class men of color often bond with white men based on patriarchal privilege even though white men do not see them as equals. They (men of color) are eager to please the father (white man) who despises him and that the man of color also despises and fears. This leads to the next section, where I invert Mexican male philosophy about *la india* and I hand it back as offensively as it has been handed to us.[28]

El Chingón: Octavio Paz and the Oedipal-Conquest-Complex

> "The worst kind of betrayal lies in making us believe that the Indian woman in US is the betrayer."
> —Gloria Anzaldúa, *Borderlands/La Frontera*

Perhaps Lacan is to French feminists what Paz is to Chicanas. Inevitably, we invoke Paz's *Labyrinth of Solitude,* where he unites us metaphorically with *La Chingada,* La Malinche.[29] We react, we respond repeatedly to his misogyny. But, misogyny alone is not what we contest. We dispute a historically specific moment which denigrates us, immortalizes us as "the betrayer" for all time, eternally stuck in an image, *la puta,* the whore. Long before the arrival of the Virgen de Guadalupe, we were *La Chingada.* The metaphor cuts to the core of each Chicana; each mestiza is flaunted as the India/whore. Worse yet is that the India is our mother and Paz slashed away at her beauty. He subordinates our first love object by violently raping her in a historical text, in male-language.

To Paz, the Aztec princess Malinche "gave" herself to Hernán Cortés, the symbol of Spanish conquest; therefore, Paz charges her with the downfall of Mexico. In Paz, we have the symbolic son, the mestizo, repudiating the symbolic father, Cortés. The Oedipal triangle is completed by *la india* that they both raped and tamed, literally and metaphorically. Malinche, the "other," the inferior, disdainful female was not worthy of marrying, so Cortés passed her down to a soldier. With the soldier, Jaramillo, Malinche bore the first mestizos. For Paz, *la india* personifies the passive whore who acquiesced to the Spaniard, the conqueror, his symbolic father—the father he despises for choosing an inferior woman who begat an inferior race, and the father he fears for his powerful phallus.

Paz's essay reveals more about his own castration complex than about Malinche. Obsessed with *chingar,* he expounds a theory to explain the inferiority complex of mestizos/as. But self-hate, the internalized racism with which Paz must contend, emanates. After all, the mighty Cortés was the white Western European male conqueror, the symbol of power that Paz was a step away from, not just as the son, but more importantly as the bastard mestizo son. Paz exhibits his own internalized racial inferiority. He holds far less power than that of his symbolic white father, *el conquistador.* On the other hand, his hatred of women, *las chingadas* and all that is female, symbolically begins with this Oedipal-conquest-triangle. Here, the sexual, political, social and psychological violence against *la india*—the core of the Chicana—is born. This core has been plundered from us through conquest and colonization. We reclaim the core for our woman-tempered *sitio y lengua.* Lacan's symbolic order of "language and meaning"[30] is epitomized in the Oedipal-conquest-triangle when the mestizo enters the pained moment of castration anxiety, but for the mestizo male the entry into the symbolic order is even more confusing because he does not know the white father's language. He cannot even guess at the meaning of symbols between himself and his conquering/colonizing father. Cultural differences divide *el español y el indio,* who were thrown together at the moment of Spanish Conquest and who misunderstand each other's symbols and language.[31]

Mestizos/as master the conqueror's language as the language of survival, but it never belongs to the conquered completely. For people whose language has been swindled twice, first the Native tongue, then the appropriated tongue, we are forced to stumble over colonizer language. As an adult, the Chicano male is perceived as the powerless son of the white Oedipal father who makes laws in his language. (African American men referred to as "boy" by white men and women reduces them to this symbolic son, but African American history of conquest and enslavement is unlike ours and I am in no position to conjecture.) Within a racist society, the mestizo male is a castrated man in relation to the white-male-colonizer father. His anxiety is not only reduced to the fear of losing it, but also to the fear that his will never match the supreme power of the white man's. While the white son has the promise of becoming the father, the mestizo, even when he becomes the father, is set apart by his skin color and by a lack of language, the dominant language of the colonizer. Moreover, he must repudiate *la india y la mestiza* for fear that he could be like her, a weak, castrated betrayer of his people. Hence, he colludes with the white-colonizer-father as they both condemn la Chicana.

The conquest triangle dictates the sexual politics of miscegenation in the twentieth century. For example, Chicanos are usually incensed when Chicanas marry the "enemy"—white men. They, on the other hand, practice male prerogative and marry white women to defy, and collaborate with, the white father, and in having half-white children move their sons a step closer to the relations of power—the white-colonizer father. For the Chicana who marries the white male, she embraces the white Oedipal colonizer ambivalently, because now she has access to power theoretically, but practically she is perceived as *la india* once again. She is not her half-white children, nor will she ever be. Her half-white sons will always have more power than she could imagine. Certainly, the same principle applies to the Chicano with a white wife, but his male privilege has already granted him rank that a Chicana cannot earn. The daughter of a white male and a Chicana has the father's white name to carry her through racist institutions, placing her closer to power relations in society.[32]

Paz's phallocratic discourse casts the Oedipal-conquest-triangle. The triangle symbolizes sociosexual-racial relations between Chicanos and Chicanas and among the white women and white men who oversee the dilemma. It is a metaphor which dictates sociosexual-racial relations. That the Oedipal moment is historically or culturally inaccurate is not the issue here. The point is that it is a symbol unconsciously perceived by Paz, who imposed the psychodrama of conquest upon the Chicano, who in turn inflicts misogyny in the image of "La Malinche" upon Chicanas/Mexicanas. But Paz cannot be held responsible for the conquest, he merely interprets history from masculinist ideology.

The law of the white-colonizer-father conditions our world in the late twentieth century. Our challenge is to rebel against the symbol of the white father and affirm our separation from his destructive ideology to create a life-affirming *sitio*. But before defying the law of the father, it is necessary to understand why we are so stuck and so addicted to the perpetrator of destruction. Why do we uphold the law of the white-colonizer-European father, knowing the extent of damage and pain for Chicanas and Chicanos? For example, Chicanos who absorb the white-colonizer father's ways hierarchically impose those laws on Chicanas. Those Chicanos become a caricature of the white-colonizer father. One has only to look at any institution where Chicanos have been integrated to see how much many of them emulate the white father and exclude women, especially women of color.[33]

Breaking the Addiction/Dependency Cycle to Patriarchal Power

> "He has no desire for woman to upset him in his sexual habits . . . his rather suspect respect for law and order. He does not want her to be anything but *his daughter,* whose gratifying fantasies of seduction it is his task to interpret, and who must be initiated into, and curbed by, the 'reasonable' discourse of his (sexual) law. Or else he wants her to be *his mother,* whose erotic reveries he would take some pleasure in hearing, whose most secret intimacy he would finally gain access to.
>
> "Unless again some very 'unconscious' *homosexual* transference is tied in there, sotto voce."
>
> —Luce Irigaray, *Speculum of the Other Woman*

In his theater production, *Corridos,* Luis Valdez reenacts a provocative *corrido* about father/daughter incest.[34] Why Valdez elected to depict this *corrido* fascinates me, but what also intrigues me is his presentation. He almost condones the arrangement, and he seems titillated by the possibility. Valdez's "Delgadina" is an insightful vehicle into the patriarchy, but more importantly, it reveals the dynamic between perpetrators and victims who create the addictive, dependent cycle between the powerful and the powerless. Like the preceding works by male centralist theorists, the production exposes Valdez's castration anxiety through his "gaze," his male definition and interpretation of the feminine.

I use the *corrido* to examine and defy Freud's "Electra complex," the inverse of the Oedipal complex. Freud hypothesized the Electra complex to explain a daughter's recognition that she cannot have her father. But just as Freud could not establish how a daughter transferred desire for her mother as her first love object to her father, so she could embrace heterosexuality, I believe, like many feminists, that he expunged patriarchal law to justify wavering transference. Hence, he rationalized his desire for the daughter's transference.

Patriarchal law dictates the tacit language and behavior of incest, which places fear in the daughter's psyche. At some point, she unconsciously recognizes the supreme phallus' potential to harm her psyche. Freud did not consider that even the remotest possibility of incest victimized the daughter. Her questions according to Freud: Does she repudiate her mother to embrace the father and to be impregnated by him as a substitute for the penis she was not born with? Does the little girl turn to the father to embrace "normal" femininity? Or, what Freud would not conjecture was her desire to remain attached to her first love object, her mother. But, wouldn't this lead to a woman-loving culture? Or worse yet, lesbianism? Wouldn't this press heterosexual women to examine their bisexual ambivalence?—their occasional desire for women while gripping the law of the father?[35]

The "Delgadina" *corrido* symbolizes a daughter's painful entrance into the law of the father. Her name *de* in Spanish, meaning "belonging to," "a man's possession," is worth nothing.

Briefly, the *corrido* tells the story of a beautiful young woman named Delgadina, whose father watches her dance by the moonlight, craves her, and then decides to pounce. As they walk home from church one day, he commands her to be his lover. When she refuses, he jails her in a tower (phallic) and waits for her to succumb. While in the tower, she is denied food and water as punishment because she disobeys the father. She begs her mother, her brother and her sister for food, water and to release her from her prison. Each one fears violating the father's order, his sexual laws, so they each ostracize Delgadina. Her mother and her sister, who are "an integral part of a phallic masculine economy,"[36] betray her. And yet, what is their alternative? For women need a moment, a specific moment of consciousness when they can separate from the law of the father into their own *sitio y lengua*. Delgadina has nowhere to turn and eventually dies from hunger for nourishment, for freedom. Her father, a broken man, is left with the memory of never having consummated sex with this young alluring love object—his daughter.

Unlike La Malinche, Delgadina does not succumb. Indeed, she dies a virgin. She is betrayed by an entire social structure that pretends, blinds itself, keeps the secret in disbelief that the father could rape his daughter, or have the desire to. But behavior and language are basic to sexual molestation. A sign, a word, a gesture can be as damaging as penetration by the penis. Patriarchal laws ignore behavior and language when litigating upon cases of molestation. For it is men who dictate that the penis must be present, armed and ready, to penetrate, and it must penetrate before male laws can consider that harm was done. For Delgadina, her psyche was penetrated.

But Valdez chose to tell us this story to peek into taboo, to peer into a "secret"—a father's sexual arousal by a young woman—his daughter. This is voyeurism, male gaze asserted. Like Hollywood's pornographic films, Valdez eroticizes women's victimization to appeal to his male audience. All this is not beside the point. To eroticize the father/daughter incestuous relationship implicitly grants permission to older men who seek young women as lovers and marriage partners. Within this relationship is the reassertion of male sexual power over a younger woman who could very likely be his daughter. Society condones the older man/younger woman relationship, in fact, envies the man who successfully catches one. A younger woman, after all, gives complete adoration, at first. Indeed, there are historical roots to older man, younger woman arrangements. In colonial California the Catholic Church and the Spanish-Mexican settlers colluded when the Church condoned marriages between older men and a niece to keep property within family.[37]

But something else occurs in the *corrido* that was sung and passed down before Valdez immortalized it. The *corrido* does not just pass down the incest taboo to warn against it. The song tells us about a young woman's death when she challenges the sexual law of the father. She cannot, however, break from the law, happy and free to join with women who believe her, or a community who will allow her to be. There is no such community. Instead, a male-centralist society with male-identified women cannot even hear her language, her pain. They just know they cannot defy the father.

But Delgadina does not have the opportunity to resist the father because by the time he commands her to be his lover, the incestuous language and behavior was in motion. The "molestation" was parodied in her perpetrator's behavior, hence leading to her "memory of molestation," which by social definition did not occur because physical touch and penis penetration did not occur. But in her memory it happened. The behavior, inappropriate for a father, to say the least, was not challenged by her mother, her sister or her brother. Not by anyone.

The addictive/dependency cycle had already begun for both of them.[38] When she tried to break from it, however, she found no support. Like Delgadina, women live in this cycle of addiction/dependency to the patriarchy that has ruled women since the precise historical moment that they become aware that women's bodies are sexually desired and/or overpowered by the penis. A young girl fears its power and tries herself to tame it, manipulate it, adore it, loathe it or ignore it, but in effect she must deal with it in some way. She may feel any variety of emotions toward the tool of oppression, but envy is not one of them. For why should she envy that which symbolically destroys?

This reminder, this memory of molestation, a memory of origin, haunts the young girl even through womanhood. Indeed, the sexual molestation memory dictates sexual desire. Either women/men repudiate the molester/perpetrator or they embrace him/her, most commonly him. Or, victims continue to repudiate and embrace the perpetrator in a persistent pattern through relationships until that addictive/dependent cycle is broken. Not until victims resist the perpetrator and have the courage to abandon the pattern, not until women and men stop assigning the perpetrator power, can women and men finally abandon phallocentric law and order.

When will those of us trying to make a revolution finally let go of these capitalist-patriarchal notions of sexual law and order which dictate a perpetrator/victim dynamic? When will we embrace the real, yet ideal notions of the collective, to work together for the common good? For within capitalist patriarchal ideology, there is no place for the sensitive human being who is willing to transform the world. "If I am the world, and I heal myself, then I heal the world." These are personal, private revolutions, each member of the collective taking responsibility for her/his contradictions within the collective, willing to grapple with the question, "Who am I exploiting?"

Both women and men are addicted to the very thing that destroys them—the patriarchy within capitalist constructs in the late twentieth century. And the social sexual relations between men and women condoned by the patriarchy are inherently unhealthy and destructive most of the time. Of course, gay men and lesbians who mimic the heterosexual arrangement inherit patriarchy's problems. The dynamic begins, I argue, in the collective memories of Western European conquerors and people of color who are subdued with the memory of the Oedipal-conquest-triangle.

To answer my question at the beginning of this essay, how are we ever to achieve a successful revolution/movement, given the strength and persistence of the patriarchy? At a certain level, the answer lies within this addictive pattern. Perhaps we must begin by modifying our behavior to change destructive patterns today, immediately, with the hope of raising children who do not have to appropriate society's addiction in order to survive. The individual is responsible to the collective, after all. To heal oneself within the collective, heals the collective. But that is only one small integral step. There is much more to do.

Un sitio y una lengua

> "But what if the 'object' started to speak? Which also means beginning to 'see,' etc."
> —Luce Irigaray, *Speculum of the Other Woman*

> "When we speak in a liberatory voice we threaten even those who may initially claim to want our words in the process of learning to speak as subjects, we participate in the global struggle to end domination."
> —bell hooks, *Talking Back*

"*Un día, mi güelita me preguntó, '¿Cómo le hablas a tu mamá, de usted o de tú?' Mi mamá le contestó, 'Yo no le enseñé de usted, 'amá.'*" Curious about their private quarrel, I witnessed how my mother defied her mother and how my grandmother questioned the manner in which her daughter raised her own daughter. Did I respect my elders in the tradition that our culture passes down through language? Or, had I become so *agringada,* so assimilated, that I spoke the disrespectful language of a younger generation so imbued with the colonizer's ways?

Like many *tejanas/os* who attended Anglo schools through grade school, I too was punished for speaking my parent's tongue on playgrounds and classrooms.[39] Spanish set my brother and me apart. Anglo teachers peered at us when we spoke Spanish, the

way white women peer at me now when they try to interfere in a
circle of Chicanas speaking together in Spanglish, reaffirming
our *mestizaje*. As a child in Anglo schools, I realized quickly that
I had to learn English, to pronounce it accurately, precisely. I was
ridiculed for my accent, I was pushed into dark closets, disci-
plined for calling a student *gringo*. I practiced at night, staring
up at the ceiling in my bedroom, reciting the alphabet. In English.
Forgetting *la lengua de mi gente*. Not knowing that the loss of
language is loss of memory. A white Lesbian feminist tells me
she is offended with my use of the word *gringa*. She tells me she
is not a *gringa*. She tells me that if I continue to use that word,
that she cannot be my friend. I think back to the *gringuitas* in my
classrooms, the ones the Anglo teachers treated with respect, the
ones who stared down at my tanned skin, the ones who ridiculed
my accent.

I rage at her arrogance. I rage at her white-skin prerogative,
her middle-class dilemma. I rage at her doctrine of reverse
racism. She tells me my rage frightens her. Can't we be polite,
womanloving about this? She has just insulted my racial memory.
Her implication: there's no room for anger in a feminist community that heals from verbal abuse. My anger about the pain and
abuse of racial violence is inappropriate when it is against her.
Why can't I take care of her and tell her kindly that she rapes my
racial memory just as a perpetrator rapes his victim. Let's do this
on my terms, in my language, in my Anglo world, she says implicitly. I'm not a *gringa*, that's a pejorative term, she shrieks.

You're a *gringa*, I thunder. You're white. You will never
know how it feels to have brown skin and a Mexican name. You
will never know what it is like to watch your mother struggle
with white words. You cannot tell me how to define who you
think you are to me. You cannot tell me what to think of you.

How many times have I lived this scene, have I repeated these
words to Anglos who invade my space, who silence my words.

My boundaries. *El Río Bravo* was once a life-giving stream that my ancestors crossed to travel north or to journey south. Back and forth, completing cycles. The river was not a boundary. *Gringos/as* built boundaries, fences, for themselves while they invaded our space, our boundaries. The boundaries that I draw to sustain my sanity. We cannot be friends as long as you think you know every part of who I am, as long as you think you can invade my space and silence my language, my thoughts, my words, my rage. *Mi sitio y mi lengua.* Invasion, a deceitful intimacy. The perpetrator wields power over the victim. The colonizer over the colonized. Sexualracial violence mirrored in language, in words. A speculum of conquest to "penetrate" further.

If discourse reveals the history of sexuality, then women of color face an obstacle. We have not had our own language and voice in history. We have been spoken about, written about, spoken at but never spoken with or listened to. Language comes from above to inflict us with western-white-colonizer ideology. We speak our history to each other now just as our ancestors used oral tradition. A tradition which is minimized. We must write in accomplished English to legitimize our work. We must master the language of the colonizer before our studies are read. *Gringos y gringas* censure our real language which is often born from rage. The colonizer's language. The French feminists do not recognize my concerns. Marguerite Duras alludes to sexual power relations between an upper-class Chinese man and a poor French girl in her novel *The Lover.*[40] Duras wrote alluring, crisp prose about a fifteen-and-one-half-year-old French girl, whose country colonized Indochina. She tells the story about the Chinese lover and the young French girl. She writes about the way her brothers, European, and older than she, disregard the Chinese man. Treat him as if he is absent, yet they take his money. She takes his money. The narrator, I suspect, recognizes this older Chinese man as an anomaly like herself. She is a woman, the only girl in her family. She is the "other." He is Chinese in a region now overrun by French colonizers. He can speak her language, French, in the colonized land. He too is the "other."

But Duras packs her story with implication. He, a man twice her age, wants sex and love with a child. She is only fifteen and one-half years old and she goes to rooms with him, sensing the differences between them, their culture, their age, but she tests first love with him, and she needs his money.

I wonder about the Chinese wife the Chinese lover marries, and how she must feel that her Chinese husband still loves the "other," the colonizer, the white skin of indulgence. We know that the narrator envisions the Chinese wife crying because her husband's heart is with the narrator, the French girl. But the Chinese woman is silent, almost absent, just a grieving consequence. She is the extreme "other," the marginal "other." She is someone who cannot understand why her husband loves this French girl. But, for me, the silence of the marginal other burns in my memory. She understands everything. The colonizer is with them in bed, the memory of white flesh pressed between them.

Sometimes, I sense that Anglo women who marry Chicanos must feel some sense of power and equality with men of color. They share an "otherness." They are not marginal others like women of color. She is a woman with white skin together with a man with brown skin. Perhaps they sense social balance in an incredibly imbalanced society. But I can only assume that, because I am neither a Chicano nor a white woman. It's only love, after all. Where do we draw boundaries in bed? In sex? How do we interpret sociosexual-racial politics in bed? Rhetorically speaking, of course.

This anxiety that *gringos* have. It is a colonizer-conqueror-anxiety, ridden with guilt about their ancestors' sins. Sometimes, some of them recognize that they inherited the sins of their fathers and mothers and those sins have afforded them this land called the Southwest, this continent called America.

Colonizer-castration-anxiety, we can even call it. They fear that Third World people will take from them what they stole and continue to steal—our language, our culture—so they can mirror themselves in us. Force us to become like them, just as the male symbolic order anxiously appropriates and denies the female for fear that he will be like her, without the powerful penis, without his dominant culture as the gauge for all others. Like eating *fajitas* at Jack-in-the-Box or nouvelle *enchiladas*. Appropriate from us to make us more palatable, to continue to conquer and colonize every piece of our differences. You are like me and I am like you. We are all human beings, they would have us believe. We are the same. Just as Irigaray points out that male culture desires a woman who mimics him, white society desires Third World people to mimic the colonizers.[41] Our land, our dignity, our rights absorbed by their omnipotent power everywhere we turn. To assuage their guilt, they want to co-opt us, make us like them. Assimilation is their best fantasy. It is best for them when we are light-skinned, but better still when Chicanos/as are half-white and half-Chicano/a. That places half-breeds closer to Anglo language and culture. But these false privileges, many recognize for what they are, a token, a *maldición*.

But to deny the penis sociosexual power, to deny the *gringo/a* cultural dominance. To revere the Chicana. To invert all power. To love myself and other Chicanas and women of color for who we have always been and continue to be. That is the revolution I speak now.

I phone my mother, I say, "Mom, *me peleé con una gringa*." "*¿Sí, hijita? Eres tan peleonera.*" She laughs. We both know she and my father taught me to fight, to have pride for a culture that *gringos* misunderstand.

When I entered the first grade, I cried each day after school. I lay my head on my mother's lap, a woman who was denied the right to read and write the language of the colonizer in a land that belonged to her ancestors. She brushed my hair back, comforting me. I couldn't articulate what I say so easily now. I couldn't say that the woman who comforted me, the woman who held power, beauty, and strength in my eyes, that Anglos dismissed her because she couldn't fill out their damn forms. I couldn't say that the school was infested with white students, so alien to me. And that day, the white teacher shoved me against a wall because I didn't recite the "Pledge of Allegiance." I didn't know it. But I knew "El Rancho Grande."

My mother would sing songs to me, Chicana lullabies. "Cielito Lindo" was my favorite. I stared up at her, making tortillas, singing. She was my *cielito lindo*. "*Canta y no llores, porque cantando te alegras, cielito lindo, mis calzones*." We sang the last word together and I giggled at what I thought was our private joke.[42]

I seek faithful allies. I have no enemies. I do not perceive white feminists, white men, heterosexuals, or even Chicano males as adversaries. But I see you, who hold sociosexual-racial power, as the subject who objectifies the marginal other me. Often, I sense you as invasive, conquering and colonizing my space and my language. You attempt to "penetrate" the place I speak from with my Chicana/Latina *hermanas*. I have rights to my space. I have boundaries. I will tell you when you cross them. I ask that you respect my request. At times, I must separate from you, from your invasion. So, call me a separatist, but to me this is not about separatism. It is about survival. I think of myself as one who must separate to my space and language of women to revitalize, to nurture and be nurtured. Then, I can resurface to build the coalitions that we must build to make the true revolution—all of us together acting the ideal, making alliances without a hierarchy of oppression. Anglo men and women, heterosexuals, white feminists, men of color, women of color, gay men, lesbians, lesbians of color, etc.

I prefer to think of myself as one who places women, especially Third World women and lesbians, in the forefront of my priorities. I am committed to women's organizations because in those spaces we revitalize, we laugh, we mock the oppressor, we mock each other's seriousness and we take each other seriously. This is a process of support, this is living the ideal, if only momentarily, to live, to nurture, to support each other in a racist, sexist, homophobic Western society. I speak at this moment as a Chicana survivor who has survived much more than I speak of here, just as we, women of color survive daily. I know that with women of color, particularly lesbians of color, I reenact the best times that I had as a child, trusting my mother and playing with my sisters and my brother while watching my father battle racism.

I give these words to you now. Like a gift. I tell you who and what I am. This is the gift I offer. Do you understand? *Ya no me van a robar mi sitio y mi lengua.* They live inside my soul, with my mother, my sisters, *mis hermanas del tercer mundo.*

But as Lacan was quick to point out, this is not the whole truth. We can only tell half-truths. No one can know all that another is. Culture denies that. The limitation of language denies that. The signifier, the object, lost in a memory, lost in colonization, but reified in my *hermandad.* We, the subjects, write; we, the subjects, speak. But do you listen? Can you hear?

QUEERING THE BORDER

Queering the Borderlands:
The Challenges of Excavating
the Invisible and Unheard

I begin with a passage from my novel in progress titled *Forgetting the Alamo, Or, Blood Memory*. I write fiction not only because I have a passion for literature, but also because I am frustrated with history's texts and archives. I've always wanted to find in the archives a queer *vaquera* from the mid-nineteenth century whose adventures include fighting Anglo squatters and seducing willing señoritas. Impaticncc lcd mc to create a *tejana* baby butch, named Micaela Campos, who must avenge her father's death at the battle of San Jacinto, just a month after the fall of the Alamo:

> By dusk she came upon the ranch and the land that her father had settled. Eleven *sitios*. Nearly forty-nine thousand acres. A lot of land for a young boy whose people had inched their way up the valley two centuries prior, moving slowly at first from the central valley then north each time the rivers shifted, each time they shifted further north to boundless prairies crossing rivers and streams. Monclova had been home for a while, two hundred years felt like plenty of time, so they picked up and moved north crossing *el Río Bravo*, traveled some more, and stopped and settled in for what they thought would be another two

hundred. They came in groups. Tlascaletecas and Otomi
with the Spanish and the Spanish with the Mexicans and
the Mexicans with Apache, mixing into a brown race jour-
neying through land expansive with blood-red horizons,
until they stopped and looked around and settled into what
was already in their blood. Movement. Settlement and
movement. Back and forth they trekked, rivers and
streams blending and interbreeding with tribes and making families and villages from beginning to end of deserts
and plains and groves. Tribes of families and villages of
mud-huts sank into the landscape where buried vessels
and bones became the soil and the clay and the water.[43]

I began with this passage in order to inscribe a gaze on the
borderlands that is geographic and spatial, mobile and impermanent. The borderlands have been imprinted by bodies that traverse the region, just as bodies have been transformed by the laws
and customs in the regions we call borderlands. In the *History of
Sexuality,* Michel Foucault challenges us to look closely at bodies and how they are engraved and transformed through laws,
customs and moralities imposed upon them through centuries.[44]
He is not as direct about coloniality, but we can still borrow from
a critique that exemplifies how land is imprinted and policed by
those traversing and claiming it as they would claim a body both
becoming property for the colonizer. Native Americans became
as much the property of the Spanish as did the land that came to
be known as the Spanish borderlands.

To unravel colonialist ideology, I put forth my notion of decolonizing history embedded in a theoretical construct that I name
the decolonial imaginary. This new category can help us rethink
history in a way that makes agency for those on the margins transformative. Colonial, for my purposes here, can be defined simply
as the rulers versus the ruled, without forgetting that those colonized may also become like the rulers and assimilate into a colo-

nial mindset. This colonial mindset believes in a normative language, race, culture, gender, class and sexuality. The colonial imaginary is a way of thinking about national histories and identities that must be disputed if contradictions are ever to be understood, much less resolved. When conceptualized in certain ways, the naming of things already leaves something out, leaves something unsaid, leaves silences and gaps that must be uncovered. The history of the United States has been circumscribed by an imagination steeped in unchallenged notions. This means that even the most radical of histories are influenced by the very colonial imaginary against which they rebel.[45] I argue that the colonial imaginary still determines many of our efforts to revise the past, to reinscribe the nation with fresh stories in which so many new voices unite to carve new disidentities, to quote Deena González and José Esteban Muñoz.[46] If we are dividing the stories from our past into categories such as colonial relations, postcolonial relations and so on, then I propose a decolonial imaginary as a rupturing space, the alternative to that which is written in history (Pérez, *The Decolonial Imaginary* 6). How do we contest the past to revise it in a manner that tells more of our stories? In other words, how do we decolonize our history? To decolonize our history and our historical imaginations, we must uncover the voices from the past that honor multiple experiences, instead of falling prey to that which is easy—allowing the white colonial heteronormative gaze to reconstruct and interpret our past.

In my own work, I have attempted to address colonial relations, of land and bodies, particularly of women, particularly of Chicanas in the Southwest. I argue that a colonial imaginary hovers above us always as we interpret our past and present. I argue that we must move into the decolonial imaginary to decolonize all relations of power, whether gendered or sexual or racial or classed (Pérez, *The Decolonial Imaginary* 6).

In my study of Chicanas, I've put forth the notion of the decolonial imaginary as a means not only of finding women who have been so hidden from history, but also as a way of honoring their agency, which is often lost. The premise that Mexican women are passive wives who follow their men had to be contested. Now, I'm asking, how is the decolonial imaginary useful for lesbian history and queer studies? If we have inherited a colonial white heteronormative way of seeing and knowing, then we must retrain ourselves to confront and rearrange a mind-set that privileges certain relationships. A colonial white heteronormative gaze, for example, will interpret widows only as heterosexual women mourning husbands. In his book, *Disidentifications: Queers of Color and the Performance of Politics,* Muñoz argues that queers of color are left out of representation in a space "colonized by the logics of white normativity and heteronormativity." For Muñoz, disidentification is the third mode of dealing with dominant ideology, one that neither opts to assimilate within such a structure nor strictly opposes it; in other words, disidentification is a strategy (11). For me, disidentification is that strategy of survival that occurs within a decolonial imaginary. In other words, the queer-of-color gaze is a gaze that sees, acts, reinterprets and mocks all at once in order to survive and to reconstitute a world where s/he is not seen by the white colonial heteronormative mind. As my queer *vaquera* baby butch gazes upon the land that her family settled upon, she is refashioning that space, re-establishing her relationship to that land as a *tejana* and as a queer who will no longer have rights to land and history. She will be erased by the white colonial heteronormative mind. And so, we will make her up or locate documents to uncover a history of sexuality on the borderlands that is hidden from the untrained eye.

How do we train the eye to see with a decolonial queer gaze that disidentifies from the normative in order to survive? The history of sexuality on and in the borderlands looks heteronormative to many historians who scrutinize marriage records, divorce records and even court cases on adultery. To disidentify is to look beyond white colonial heteronormativity to interpret documents differently.

Historians have explored race, class, gender, ethnicity and nation, region; however, sexuality and more specifically, queer history, has only recently joined the ranks of serious scrutiny. Generally, historians of sexuality in the United States and Europe have offered key books and articles that examine the lives of women and men in New York, Buffalo, London, San Francisco and even the South. For example, historians like Martin Duberman, Martha Vicinus, George Chauncy Jr., Elizabeth Lapovsky Kennedy, Madeline D. Davis, Lillian Faderman, Randolph Trumbach, Lisa Duggan and John Howard uncover queer histories in the United States and Britain while the Southwest borderlands is quite nearly untouched.[47] Historical studies that focus upon Chicanas/os and Mexicans of the Southwest primarily highlight immigrant and labor studies, social histories of communities and biographies of heroes or heroines. The study of gender and sexuality, however, is central in works by Deena González, *Refusing the Favor: The Spanish Mexican Women of Santa Fe, 1820-1880;* Ramón Gutiérrez, *When Jesus Came, the Corn Mothers Went Away: Marriage, Sexuality, and Power in New Mexico, 1500-1846;* and Antonia Castañeda, "Sexual Violence in the Politics and Policies of Conquest: Amerindian Women and the Spanish Conquest of Alta California."[48] Queer histories of the Southwest and of the US-Mexico borderlands are that much more marginal; however, there are as many questions as there are sources for interrogation. Cultural and literary texts, newspapers, police records, widows' wills, court dockets, medical records, texts by sexologists, religious tracts, as well as *corridos*—all of these and more must be reinterpreted with a decolonial queer gaze so we may interrogate representations of sexual deviants and track ideologies about sex and sexuality.

We must begin by asking: For whom and by whom has sexuality been defined? Who was having sex with whom when laws began to police the practice of sex? Foucault contends that discourses of sex and sexuality, specifically the history of those discourses in Europe, were transformed from somewhat more libratory in the eighteenth century to far more repressive in the nineteenth century. Victorian England made a space in which deviant sexualities could be repressed on the one hand and could proliferate on the other (Foucault 3-4). The mixed scheme of moralities spread through the Western world, and the borderlands between Mexico and the United States were no exception, particularly after the US-Mexico War of 1846-48, when droves of white Anglo Saxon Protestants brought with them a white colonial heteronormative ideology. Sexuality, then, cannot be defined without attention to epochs and centuries, each of which imprinted borderland queers in its own way. Racialized sexualities on the geographic border we know as El Paso del Norte has its own underpinning, however.

An examination of the late-nineteenth and early-twentieth centuries on the border of El Paso/Juárez offers one window into twenty-first-century lesbian and queer identities. (I use each term of identity cautiously, given that each identity is charged with its own politics and history. While "queer" has for many become the overarching identity for all who are nonheteronormative, "lesbian" is sustained as the self-identity for women who choose to be with other women-physically, psychically and politically.) The late-nineteenth and early-twentieth centuries are key for a couple of reasons. One reason is that the late-nineteenth century is encoded with Victorian values of repressive sexuality. Sex acts became policed in ways they had not been before. In her book *Queering the Color Line: Race and the Invention of Homosexuality in American Culture,* Siobhan B. Somerville argues that "it is not historical coincidence that the classification of bodies as either homosexual or heterosexual emerged at the same time that the United States was aggressively constructing and policing the boundaries between black and white bodies."[49] Somerville refers to the 1896 Supreme Court case, *Plessy v. Ferguson,* which established a "separate but equal clause" that legalized the segregation of blacks from whites. I would further note that in the Southwest, in these geographic borderlands, *Plessy v. Ferguson* sanctioned the segregation of brown from white.

Moreover, I would take her premise and argue further that it is not historical coincidence that the classifications of homosexual and heterosexual appeared at the same time that the United States began aggressively policing the borders between the United States and Mexico. The change from the Texas Rangers, who policed Indian and Mexican territory in the nineteenth century, to the Border Patrol, created in 1924 to police the border between the United States and Mexico, occurred at the moment when a new form of anti-Mexican sentiment emerged throughout the nation. The sentiment was linked to anti-immigrant acts that would become laws against non-Northern Europeans. As the borders in Texas, California, Arizona and New Mexico were pushed against by too many Mexicans crossing the *Río Bravo*, trekking back and forth through land they had crossed for centuries and paying little attention to anything but rising river banks, the borders become more and more closed and only opened up when a labor shortage demanded cheap laborers. Meanwhile, a brown race was legislated against from fear that it could potentially infect the purportedly pure, white race in the United States. Eugenicists and sexologists, according to Somerville, worked hand in hand (Sommerville, *Queering the Color Line* 31).

Consequently, the border was closed as a result of scientific racism clouded by a white colonial heteronormative gaze looking across a river to see racial and sexual impurities. Throughout the 1880s, 1890s and even as late as the 1900s, Mexicans crossed from Juárez to El Paso and back again with ease. Not until 1917 did a law impose requirements on those crossing a political border. A head tax of eight dollars per person and the ability to read restricted the crossings.[50] I would ask: How did the emergent and rigid policing of the border between the United States and Mexico in the early twentieth century reinforce a white colonial heteronormative way of seeing and knowing that fused race with sex? Further investigation will illustrate that the ideologies constructed around race and sex were linked to justify who was undesirable as a citizen in the United States. Immoral and deviant behavior included anything that was not a heterosexual marriage between a woman and man. In the El Paso of 1891, adultery could lead to the arrest of both man and woman. Of course, someone would have to file a complaint to have them arrested, usually an unhappy third party. The courts listened and adjudicated many cases of adultery in which Mexican women and men were thrown into jail because they "unlawfully live together and have carnal intercourse" outside of marriage.[51]

Another way of tackling primary research for an "invisible" group is to study the category of "deviance" and how deviant behavior has become a politicized queer identity in the twenty-first century. It is not a coincidence that Chicana lesbian historian Deena González unearthed the lives of widows, or women who lived alone during the nineteenth century.[52] González was already thinking outside and beyond a heteronormative interpretation when she perused nineteenth-century documents.

Oral interviews and ethnography are the methods available to those who do not want to ferret through pre-twentieth-century tracts to find queer histories. For the late twentieth century, activist-scholar Yolanda Retter has conducted extensive research on the lesbian communities of Los Angeles from the 1970s through to the 1990s, relying on oral interviews, as did Kennedy and Davis. Chicana lesbian historian Yolanda Chavez Leyva has also conducted a series of oral interviews on the lives of Chicana lesbian activists in Tucson, Arizona. Sociologist Deborah Vargas has interrogated queer audience responses to *tejana* singer/performer Selena and the drag artists posing as Selena. Theorist and historian Maylei Blackwell has interviewed a Chicana feminist activist from the 1970s who was ostracized from the Chicano movement because she was a feminist, meaning a lesbian to many homophobic Chicanos in the early movement.[53]

Chicana lesbian cultural critics Luz Calvo, Catriona Esquibel, Sandra Soto, Yvonne Yarbro-Bejarano and others continue to problemetize how we think of queers in, on and of many borders.[54] The border *reina,* Gloria Anzaldúa, could not have known the impact her book of poetry and essays would have on the field called Borderlands, which was initially coined the "Spanish Borderlands" in the early twentieth century by University of California historian Herbert Eugene Bolton.[55] Studies by queer cultural critics and theoreticians influenced by Anzaldúa's work continue to proliferate. Creative writers have also been theorizing the borderlands and its deviant, non-normative population for the last few decades. In her historical novel, El Paso border writer Alicia Gaspar de Alba's queering of Sor Juana Inez de la Cruz has caused consternation among those who cannot imagine a nun having sex with another woman. Many of Gaspar de Alba's short stories are reflections of the border twin cities of El Paso and Ciudad Juárez. Other border queer writers, like John Rechy and Arturo Islas, also from El Paso, construct powerful narratives in which their protagonists confront heteronormative sexuality.[56]

Historical research on and of borderland queers is not as abundant. Part of the problem is that the queer gaze has only recently become sanctioned. Queer history, after all, is a new, growing field. Despite the practice of queering our daily lives, academic institutions and disciplines have discouraged that "oh so disturbing" queer gaze. Our epistemological shift, however, has already begun to challenge rhetoric and ideologies about racialized sexualities. To queer the border is to look at the usual documents with another critical eye, a nonwhite, noncolonial, nonheteronormative eye. A decolonial queer gaze would permit scholars to interrogate medical texts, newspapers, court records, wills, novels and *corridos* with that fresh critical eye. Graduate

students at the University of Texas at El Paso (UTEP) are scrutinizing some of these records in order to construct the queer history of the border. In the History Department, I offered for the
first time a graduate seminar on "Gender and Sexuality on the
Border," in which queer history was explored. In the seminar,
graduate students conducted research on El Paso/Juárez, tracking gay, lesbian and queer histories through the centuries. Because the majority of historical studies on gender and sexuality
ignore the geographic border between the United States and Mexico, these graduate students and I realized that it is difficult to assess how to pursue research on queers in this region. We also
concluded that "queer" history included anyone who was considered "deviant," therefore we expanded whom we studied and
how we conducted our studies. We found ourselves "queering"
the documents. This was a daunting task; however, the students
were creative as they challenged white heteronormative sexualities in studies that explored, for example, Juárez *transvestis* in
their workplace, prostitution in the late nineteenth and early twentieth centuries, lesbian oral histories of the El Paso community,
gay and lesbian activists of El Paso and Mexican-American
women's agency in the *colonias* of El Paso. Some of these studies are ongoing. UTEP's Ph.D. program in Borderlands History,
the only one of its kind in the nation, is regionally specific to the
United States and Mexico, and therefore is drawing students of
color who are Chicana/o and Mexican nationals. A core faculty in
the department is training students whose research interests include gender/sexuality/race/ethnicity in the borderlands, the Mexican Revolution, histories of Colonial Mexico, the Southwest,
Latin America and Spain, as well as comparative world borders.

But what about the gaps and silences? I know that nineteenth-
century *tejanas* lived and roamed the "Wild West" and probably
knew how to handle a six-shooter and ride a horse, and I'm sure
there were those who passed as men and those who loved women.
As much as I would love to stumble upon diaries, journals and

letters written by queer *vaqueras* of the nineteenth century, I must challenge my own desire for the usual archival material and the usual way of seeing, as well as honor that which women scholars before me have uncovered. While I will not always find the voices of the subaltern, the women, the queers of color, I will have access to a world of documents rich with ideologies that enforce white, colonial heteronormativity. A white heteronormative imaginary has defined how researchers and historians as well as cultural critics have chosen to ignore or negate the populations who are on the margins, outside of normative behavior, outside of twentieth-century nuclear, white, heterosexual family systems. I am arguing for a decolonial queer gaze that allows for different possibilities and interpretations of what exists in the gaps and silences but is often not seen or heard. I am arguing for decolonial queer interpretations that obligate us to see and hear beyond a heteronormative imaginary. I am arguing for decolonial gendered history to take us into our future studies with perspectives that do not deny, dismiss, or negate what is unfamiliar, but instead honors the differences between and among us.

Gloria Anzaldúa: La Gran Nueva Mestiza
Theorist, Writer, Activist-Scholar

Once when I met Gloria for dinner in Santa Cruz, she looked at me with a glint in her eye and said, *"Te ves bien butchona."* I was so pleased with her compliment that shortly after that evening, I went shopping for more butch-like attire. A Chicana *jota* whom I respected had encouraged me after all. I'm sure it wasn't a coincidence that I ran into Gloria at the Gap when I bought my favorite blue work shirt in the men's department. I've had that shirt for nearly a decade. What was once blue is now faded powder blue. The cuffs are frayed, the pockets ripped, yet I refuse to throw it away. Not until recently, when I remembered that Gloria had been present the day I bought that shirt, did I realize why I still need to see it hanging in my closet. The shirt reminds me of the playful glint in Gloria's eye.

Gloria had a way of influencing her friends, her *comadres,* her admirers and followers into new kinds of liberatory consciousness in quiet, subtle ways. Every time with Gloria felt like a subtle lesson in her theories and her routine practice of those theories. In retrospect, running into her at the Gap, one of her favorite places to shop, held metaphoric implications that only recently became obvious to me. Gloria had already theorized that in between space, that unseen, forgotten, unspoken place she often referred to as *"Nepantla,"* the Nahuatl word/concept for that ambiguous, tentative, ever-changing space we all inhabit.

Significantly, Gloria also fused contemporary queer conceptions with the Nahuatl concept of duality, that is, exhibiting both female and male qualities. She not only understood the cultural insinuations of butch-femme identities, but she also reaffirmed those cultural manifestations through her idiom, *mita' y mita'*, half and half. She pointed out, "I, like other queer people, am two in one body, both male and female. I am the embodiment of the *hieros gamos:* the coming together of opposite qualities within" (*Borderland/La Frontera* 1987, 19). Long before the burgeoning studies on female masculinity, Gloria argued that queers "are not suffering from a confusion of sexual identity, or even from a confusion of gender" (19). For her, present-day society limited human beings by imposing rigid roles, a "despotic duality," rather than avowing that humans can evolve, can be better.

I'd like to address some of her more prominent theories and the manner in which her theories have not only influenced my day-to-day life but have also transformed my academic work.

La Conciencia de la Mestiza

Decades ago Gloria Anzaldúa comprehended what many of us spend our lives attempting to grasp—that colonization may have destroyed our indigenous civilizations but colonization could not eliminate the evolution of an indigenous psyche. That world still persists inside our community's psychic, material lives. We wear it on our bodies, our flesh, our *mestizaje.* The mixed racial bodies and minds that we've inherited usher that past into the present and, more important, into the future. She devised her theory—*la conciencia de la mestiza*—as a method, a tool that offered us hope to move from a bleak present into a promising future. *La conciencia de la mestiza,* mestiza consciousness, is that transformative tool (81). She said:

> The work of mestiza consciousness is to break down
> the subject-object duality that keeps her a prisoner and to

show in the flesh and through the images of her work how duality is transcended. The answer to the problem between the white race and the colored, between males and females, lies in healing the split that originates in the very foundation of our lives, our culture, our languages, our thoughts . . . collective consciousness is the beginning of a long struggle, but one that could, in our best hopes, bring us to the end of rape, of violence, of war. (*Borderlands* 80)

For Gloria, mestiza consciousness must be attained by all races, by all people. It is the consciousness that we need to take us through the twenty-first century, from *el quinto sol* (the fifth sun) to *el sexto sol* (the sixth sun). The Aztec and Maya calendars both prophesied the ending of war and violence with the ending of the fifth sun. The transition from the fifth to the sixth sun began in 1988 and will be completed in 2012. Gloria passed on during those pivotal transitional years between the suns, only eight years before the fifth sun fully completed its cycle to begin the transition into the sixth sun. The sixth sun will bring harmony, peace and justice. To quote Gloria, mestiza consciousness will guide us toward "the creation of yet another culture" and to "a new value system with images and symbols that connect us to each other and the planet" (81). The "clash of cultures" will become embedded in our very flesh. The consciousness of our crossbreeding will create a culture of harmony, where love and hope become key. Moreover, the crossbreeding of cultures occurs, for Gloria, in the borderlands.

Borderlands: Psychic, Sexual, Political, Geographic

In the preface to *Borderlands/La Frontera: The New Mestiza*, Gloria Anzaldúa began her powerful work with the following paragraph:

The actual physical borderland that I'm dealing with in this book is the Texas-U.S. Southwest/Mexican border. The psychological borderlands, the sexual borderlands and the spiritual borderlands, are not particular to the Southwest. In fact, the Borderlands are physically present wherever two or more cultures edge each other, where people of different races occupy the same territory, where under, lower, middle and upper classes touch, where the space between two individuals shrinks with intimacy. (1987, preface)

In that opening paragraph, she illustrated complexities that scholars continue to debate, reiterate, draw from, extrapolate, deconstruct and reconstruct. In essence, Gloria Anzaldúa forged a new territory, a new intellectual locale, a new spiritual space, a new psychic and psychological terrain. She created fresh symbols, metaphors and taxonomies to describe a material world where poverty, racism, homophobia are real problems and where a psychic, sacred inner world is as real as the material, tangible world. For her there were no boundaries. She leapt across borders between the real and imaginary because she knew that one could inhabit both at once. In addition, she theorized what it was like to be a queer of color who not only inhabited sexual borderlands, but also survived sexual borderlands that often terrorized queers. Herself a queer of color, *una jota, una marimacha de la frontera,* she spoke about the pain and the creativity of living between worlds, of melding the real and metaphoric borderlands. In her essay, "To(o) Queer the Writer," published many years after her path-breaking book, *Borderlands/La Frontera,* Anzaldúa took issue with criticism that dismissed her queer convictions, which were always already meshed with interrogations of race, sex/gender and class (Anzaldúa 1998). Her writings illustrate that she has always lived between many worlds and to expect her work to reflect only one world or one identity was false. As a queer Chicana from south Texas, Anzaldúa inhabited multiple identities at once, just as we all do, and she reminded us that our movement between and among these borderlands was necessary for our cultural and political survival. To say that Gloria was not queer enough in her writings is to negate her theorizing of the sexual borderlands. She argued that queers of color in the borderlands navigate a politically charged and racialized terrain in which harsh violence is always a danger. Perhaps because she offered theories, concepts and philosophies for everyone's daily struggles, not only queers, not only Chicanas, her work has been taken up by many who understand her collective appeal. The following concepts are especially significant.

Transforming Theories: Nepantla, Coatlicue State, la Facultad, Shadow Beast

Anzaldúa's many concepts evolved from an astute awareness of what it meant to live in between worlds—mestiza consciousness itself is the road through *Nepantla* with *la facultad* while haunted by the shadow beast and coping with the *Coatlicue* state, attempting to befriend it to reach finally yet another intense stage of mestiza consciousness. The road is cyclical, like Maya and Aztec time, moving in circles but each movement further and deeper into yet another level of consciousness.

I wasn't aware of how profoundly important *Nepantla,* that in between space, was to her way of seeing until I took a walk with her on the beach in Santa Cruz. I can't remember exactly the year; I just know that I was in San Francisco and drove to Santa Cruz to spend time with her. It was early evening and she asked me if I wanted to take a walk with her. Since I too love the ocean, I consented, and we strolled from her house to the water. The sun began to set and we continued walking along the boardwalk talking about nothing in particular. She might have asked about whomever I was dating at the time, and I think she even offered some advice since she knew the woman I was seeing better than I did. Let me point out that Gloria's intuitive sensibility, what she would call her *Coatlicue* state, seemed to rear its head quite often, and she always knew more, sensed more, than I could or did at

the time. I often felt like a novice when I was with her and she
was the patient, loving teacher/friend. Anyway, I might have
probed about her love life, but she hardly ever spent much time
discussing that with me. Maybe she saved that topic for more familiar friends. As the sun disappeared beyond the horizon, the
light began to change. Golden sun and shadows fell away and
suddenly a bluish tone absorbed the air. It was neither light nor
dark. We could still see in front of us, but all objects were encir-
cled with a shadowy, indigo aura. I became somewhat annoyed
because my vision tends to deceive me at dusk. She, on the other
hand, said, "You see this light; it's light, but it's also dark. It's in
between night and day. My favorite time of day. When it's night-
time and daytime at once." I'd never focused on the light at dusk
before, other than to want it to hurry up and change from one to
the other. I realized at that moment that I had always been un-
comfortable with that ambiguity. Suddenly, as if to see for the
first time, I became aware of living between worlds, between
seemingly opposites. I became aware of *Nepantla*. It was a significant lesson for this student because I would think about this
again and again for years to come, and as I theorized Chicana/o
history, I used her concept of the in between to make sense of
what I call the decolonial imaginary—that space between colonial and postcolonial. For me, Gloria's *Nepantla* concept allowed
me to think about the liberatory space that Chicanas/os exist in
today. Neither colonial nor postcolonial, we reside in that in between gap where we make sense of our agency.

Coatlicue State

The *Coatlicue* state is a psychic sensibility, one that we ignore
or dismiss in our post-Enlightenment Western European training.
I have to admit I never permitted myself to quite grasp what she
meant by the *Coatlicue* state. I was, after all, trained in the 1970s
and 1980s when a feminist and Marxist materialist critique su-

perseded all others. Not until now as I read and reread *Border-lands/La Frontera* did I realize, of course, the battle within. She had always been referring to that inner struggle in which cultural identity is inextricably enmeshed with ambiguity. But an ambiguity that allows for degrees of differences, for shifting and moving around inside another perspective, a third perspective—not a static one—but a mobile cultural identity that is always already transforming. For me, the *Coatlicue* state allows me to tap into an intuitiveness that helps me survive daily. Like *la facultad,* which is the interpretive tool, the *Coatlicue* state is that space in which we dwell when we plunge into the abyss of self-pity, of *borracheras* without alcohol or drugs. The *Coatlicue* state is the alternate consciousness that we delve into, feeling sorry for ourselves until *Coatlicue* kicks our butt and says, *"Ya. Párale."* Time to move on, to get through this, to learn from all you have experienced in your material and psychic worlds. It's that crucial time when we're haunted by the shadow beast, our inner selves, that part that won't let us rest, that part that says, you're never going to meet the ideal expected of you. I call my own shadow beast that ego-driven, maniacal, Eurocentric-minded part of me immersed in inner battle. When I'm so exhausted by my own inner demons, I call upon *la facultad* to assist me so that I may delve into the *Coatlicue* state to recover a sense of humility, to recover a sense of cultural, psychic identity. There is a kind of self-therapy that is so much a part of Gloria's concepts, but her theories are more than self-therapy. Gloria's theories, when applied, call upon us to transform not only ourselves but also our many communities.

Decolonial Theorist

Elsewhere, I discuss the significance of *Borderlands/La Frontera* and its impact upon Chicana history and cultural studies (see *The Decolonial Imaginary* 1999). Borderlands had already been conceptualized by the prominent historiography school of the Spanish Borderlands at University of California, Berkeley by Herbert Eugene Bolton in the 1920s and 1930s (Bolton 1915). The historiography school was important because it opened the eyes of the East coast scholars who were compelled finally to see that the United States had attained or rather colonized a region formerly Spanish, formerly Mexican, formerly Native American. But like so many historiography schools of thought from the early twentieth century, this one too disregarded women, whether Euroamerican, Irish, Spanish, Spanish-Mexican, or Native American. Not until the late twentieth century, with the publication of *Borderlands/La Frontera,* did that omission become remedied in a way that traditional scholars/historians would never have imagined. Gloria's book, after all, is conscious myth-making, conscious interpretive narrative that re-centers *la India y la Mestiza.* Criticized by traditional historians who did not understand the creative impulse to move beyond Eurocentric Western European thinking, Gloria's scholarly study set up new borderlands. Her book became the progression toward postmodern, postnational identities for Chicanas/mestizas. She reinscribed *Borderlands/La Frontera,* and those terms became the keywords, the metaphoric lynchpins for many late twentieth and early twenty-first century writings. As a Chicana feminist theoretician, she intervened with a treatise that presented history as only another literary genre. Debates circulated about the book's historical errors, but many more traditional historians simply missed the metaphor and read too literally—as we often can.

Anzaldúa's conscious myth-making opened a site for gendered discourse about *la nueva mestiza* and her central location in the borderlands. Hers was a cutting-edge perspective that changed Chicana/o studies despite the fact that it is held suspect in the academy because she ventures beyond the confines of the academy's authorized debates. She moved into unexpected territory, daring to risk lines of inquiry and, like Michel Foucault, interrogated existing discursive fields. She moved beyond the

Chicano nationalist project and issued a postnationalist feminist project in which *la nueva mestiza,* the mixed-race woman, is the privileged subject of that in between space, that interstitial space that was formerly a nation and must be without borders, without boundaries. She challenged Chicano nationalist discourse and critiqued the discursive nation as a space that negates feminists, queers (*jotas y jotos*) *and* anyone who is not of "pure" Chicano blood or lineage. *Mestizaje,* for Anzaldúa, is redefined and remixed into an open consciousness where "racial, ideological, cultural and biological cross-pollination" co-exist (77).

Decolonial Queer Theorist

Published in 1981, *This Bridge Called My Back: Writings by Radical Women of Color* opened up a path for women-of-color writers, activists and theorists (Moraga and Anzaldúa). Women like Gloria meshed their political lives with their scholarly and community lives. The voices, especially the queer of color voices in the anthology, spoke to me in ways that no other writings had before.

Published before any of the contemporary studies on queers in the last decade, Gloria Anzaldúa and Cherrie Moraga had already offered *This Bridge Called My Back* to fill a gap felt and known and lived by many of us. After perusing the essays in *This Bridge,* most of us figured out quite quickly that the radical women of color were for the most part, lesbians of color. Moreover, the essays in the anthology spoke from a queer/lesbian-of-color position that melded race, sex and class. The authors were some of the first who published testimonials about the effects of living in a majority white, heteronormative world. More than any other text from the last few decades, *This Bridge Called My Back* articulated what I refer to as a decolonial critical stance, meaning it was oppositional at the same time that it was negotiating between what had been inherited—a history of racism, homophobia, coloniality—and what was being contested and decolonized—racism, homophobia, coloniality—and what was hoped for—the end of racism, homophobia, coloniality, hence the move toward postcoloniality. Six years later, when Anzaldúa published *Borderlands/La Frontera,* she referred to herself as *jota,* or queer. As she theorized what it meant to be *la nueva mestiza,* she argued that as a Chicana *jota* from the border and from another generation, she had never felt comfortable with the self-identifying term, lesbian, but instead had grown up with "queer" and all its negative connotations yet still embraced it because it was and is what made sense to her. My point in offering this information is to confirm that as a queer of color, Anzaldúa had been theorizing queerness from a decolonial perspective in which issues of race and coloniality were always already enmeshed in her writing.

Conclusion

When I attended the Texas Lesbian conference held in Houston in 1989, *Borderlands/La Frontera* had been published two years prior, and Gloria was the keynote speaker. I was living in Houston at the time. So I was compelled to attend. After her talk, I made sure to approach her, introduce myself and ask her to sign my copy of *Borderlands/La Frontera.* As soon as I confessed that I was a fellow *Tejana,* she turned her attention to me, gave me her phone number, her address and told me to visit her when I was back in California. I don't remember all the times we spoke or visited, but a few times do stick out in my mind, and I think they do because like that time when I saw her at the Gap, she said something or looked a certain way that coached me into some other level of consciousness. There was a walk on the beach, not far from her house in Santa Cruz, there were her homemade tamales at her apartment also in Santa Cruz, there was the visit to Claremont when she spent a month as a visiting scholar at the Claremont Colleges near Los Angeles, and she cooked with so many spices I can't remember them all. There was her visit to University of California, Santa Barbara where Chela Sandoval and I spent days with her at Chela's condominium in Santa Barbara, tracking down the latest holistic medicine on diabetes. All those times are memorable and each time was a seminar, a calm, subtle, wise tutorial in mestiza consciousness, *Nepantla, la facultad,* as well as the *Coatlicue* state.

To write about someone you love who has passed on is never easy. To attempt to honor that someone's memory with words is even more difficult especially when you continue to love this person, this larger-than-life theorist, writer, activist-scholar named Gloria Anzaldúa. *La gran nueva mestiza* was a friend, a mentor and an intellectual companion. The day I heard about her passing, I did what many of us did; I immediately chose to believe that it couldn't be true, that someone had made a mistake. I had just left a conference on Queer Latinidad at the University of Chicago and while waiting at the Chicago airport, I checked my cell phone messages and I heard a garbled message from a close friend who shares with me love and respect for Gloria. Given that the message was indistinguishable, I denied what I thought I'd heard until I arrived home and saw an e-mail from many friends assuring that the news of her death was indeed true. Gloria had passed on in her home in Santa Cruz, near the ocean that she loved so much.

Memories of my private time with her have been playing over and over in my head, and I know I have refused to believe she's gone. Having to write these things down, having to remember her and opting to share those memories has brought me closer to acknowledging her death. But death—that Western European concept—is not befitting of Gloria. Gloria would not have believed that passing to that next dimension was death for her. She would have believed that she was on her next journey, into the next realm of borderlands, into yet another unseen province of *Nepantla.*

How will we choose to remember someone who has made
lasting imprints upon our global communities? Gloria's work,
after all, is the prime example of border-crossing. Her writing has
crossed oceans and disciplines. I remember a story she told me
about a middle-aged, white, male, German scholar who appeared
one day at her mother's doorstep in south Texas, intentionally
seeking information about this brilliant philosopher theorist
named Gloria Anzaldúa. She said that her family had never
known her growing notoriety until that German scholar's visit.
Unfortunately, the US academy took its time acknowledging the
power and magnitude of her concepts. Many of us picked up her
ideas and refused to allow them to be marginalized just as we
will not allow her ideas to be forgotten. International scholars
and communities continue to cite her work, continue to make
links across borders and boundaries that only serve to separate
us. Germans, Españoles, Mexicanas/os, the Dutch, southeast
Asians and so many more across the globe have read and studied
Gloria's inspirational words. It's astounding when you stop to
think that a *chicanita, prietita, jotita del valle de tejas* has made
an indelible mark upon the global community.

Long after the end of this century, her philosophy will en-
dure. Gloria was an unassuming philosopher-poet whose words
will inspire generations. She articulated our past to make sense of
our present; however, she didn't just look to Nahuatl culture because she was merely seeking origins. She looked to that past to
excavate hope for our future.

In one of the last sections of *Borderlands/La Frontera,* Gloria discusses her obsession, her need to write and to do so daily.
She says,

> I sit here before my computer, Amiguita, my altar on
> top of the monitor with the Virgen de Coatlalopeuh can-
> dle and copal incense burning. My companion, a wooden
> serpent staff with feathers, is to my right while I ponder

the ways metaphor and symbol concretize the spirit and etherealize the body. The Writing is my whole life, it is my obsession. This vampire which is my talent does not suffer other suitors. Daily I court it, offer my neck its teeth. This is the sacrifice that the act of creation requires, a blood sacrifice. For only through the body, through the pulling of flesh, can the human soul be transformed. And for the images, words, stories to have this transformative power, they must arise from the human body—flesh and bone—and from the Earth's body—stone, sky, liquid, soil. This work, these images, piercing tongue or ear lobes with cactus needle, are my offerings, are my Aztecan blood sacrifices. (75)

Her work, her images and offerings will continue to transform us and the generations that succeed us. *Gracias, Gloria por tus palabras, tus grandes ideas y teorías, tu humanidad y, más que nada, tu esperanza.*

It's Not about the Gender in My Nation, But about the Nation in My Gender: The Decolonial Virgen in a Decolonial Site

"Chicano/a desire for a brown-skinned Guadalupe is formed in and through the social and historical institutionalization of racial hierarchies, a direct result of the colonization of the Americas and its enduring racial legacies. However, the imagined collective allegiance to a sexless brown mother has come at considerable cost: women's active sexuality."[57]

Alma Lopez's digital print titled, "Our Lady," offers a decolonial methodology for Chicanas who have reclaimed La Virgen de Guadalupe and reinscribed her with queer desire and pleasure. The passage at the beginning of my essay exemplifies a decolonial critique of traditional gender roles pervasive in colonial, patriarchal ideologies. The ideology is one that promotes a virgin/whore dichotomy that remains integrated in Latino/a culture. And because Lopez's digital print complicates the virgin/whore binary, a controversy ensued in the Chicano nation.

In her essay, "Art Comes for the Archbishop: The Semiotics of Contemporary Chicana Feminism and the Work of Alma Lopez,"[58] Chicana feminist theorist Luz Calvo reasons that the making of la Virgen de Guadalupe depended upon a colonial moment in the Americas, coloniality that perpetuates the Chicano nationalist desire for demure, passive brown women who emulate the nation's brown virgin. Calvo's premise contests the ideology espoused in colonial patriarchal culture. Commenting on Alma Lopez's digital collage, "Our Lady," the feminist theorist maintains that controversy pursues Lopez's representation of La Virgen de Guadalupe precisely because women, especially Latinas and Chicanas, are not permitted to be active, sexed subjects of their own lives. History and its colonizing institutions have not allowed brown women to be active subjects. If however, women break out of a passive, sexless role, they are deemed "bad" women. There are, after all, only two types of women: the "bad" woman in the street with whom a man may carouse and spend the night and the "good woman" at home to whom he is married. Good women should not be in the street carousing. Instead, they must be condemned to virginal goodness and greet husbands cheerfully regardless of their many exploits.

With Spain's invasion of the Americas, a colonial mind-set that mirrored Eurocentric gender-roles was installed. I have argued that the Chicano/a community inherited the virgin/whore binary that was imposed upon the "new world" through the religious icon, La Virgen de Guadalupe and through La Malinche, or, Malintzin Tenepal, known historically as Hernán Cortés's whore.[59] Shortly before Cortés journeyed to Tenochtitlan in 1519, Malinche had already been sold as a slave by her own parents. Offered as a gift to Cortés along with twenty-one other Indian maidens, the young woman became an indispensible translator to the Spanish conqueror. By 1521, the conquest of Tenochtitlan was complete and ten years later the brown virgin appeared to the Indian Juan Diego on Tepeyac hill. Scholars have noted that the growing mestizo population of the "new" world rejected Spain's white Mary compelling the Catholic Church to offer the newly colonized people a brown virgin with whom they could identify.[60] Interestingly, the virgin/whore dichotomy emerged in colonial Mexico's 16th century as a colonial construction that would inhabit the lives of mestizos and mestizas into the twenty-first century. It has taken Chicana feminists to undo this colonial binary that continues to trouble contemporary gender roles.

The Chicana lesbian artist, Alma Lopez, has provided a window into deconstructing the meaning of a paramount cultural icon in Chicano/a communities that has been used to perpetuate problematic gender expectations. When Lopez deliberately departs from a traditional depiction of "Our Lady," she submits knowingly an intervention that calls upon audiences to revitalize the image with new meanings. In this instance, the Virgin stands in a rather provocative floral bikini compelling spectators to think about her as a real, living, loving, sexed, desiring woman. Spectators, especially Chicana lesbians spectators, take pleasure from gazing upon Lopez's rendering. And that pleasure, pronounced unabashedly, is as improper as it is offensive to the patriarchal Chicano nation.

I would like to examine some of the protest language sparked against "Our Lady" when Santa Fe's Museum of International Folk Art exhibited the digital artwork in 2001. What the discourse of protest shows is that the New Mexican Chicano/a community, who opposed the piece, believed that only they controlled the "true" meaning of the Virgin. Ironically, their discursive turn demonstrated how the protestors themselves, not the artist, were the ones who inflicted an overly sexualized virgin in the people's imagination. By "putting sex into discourse" and "speaking of it ad infinitum,"[61] the protesters attempted to guard la Virgen from sexuality. Virgins, after all, must remain virgins. But while their language calls for the Virgin's protection against sexual innuendo, women in general were also addressed. A close look at the discourse reveals how women are once again prohibited from being sexual, desiring subjects. As a result, the discourse that emerged from the exhibit sought to silence a specific Chicana lesbian but also to control women in general.

When examining the protestor's letters to the artist, I was not surprised that the most vociferous, persistent dissenters were men; however, the women who practice devout community, regional Catholicism representative of *nuevomejicano* tradition and history, also criticized Lopez's "Our Lady." As a result, the artwork itself could not be seen as an intervention for Chicanas who challenge how the Chicano nation has marked them as colonial objects with no agency, no desire and no right to be "desiring subjects." Instead, the "imagined collective allegiance to a sexless brown mother," as Calvo points out, was grasped and enforced.

My analysis probes the necessity of decolonizing the minds of a community ruled by historical colonial relationships that continue to stamp contemporary lives and culture. How do we decolonize our community's perspectives about La Virgen de Guadalupe? Public ownership is seemingly patriarchal, I would argue, and as a result a patriarchal order of things is enforced not only by men but also by women. But the manner in which men and women prop up a patriarchal order is distinct. Moreover, particular Chicano nationalist politics are far more invested in sustaining traditional, colonial perceptions of La Virgen rather than decolonizing those images. I'll say more about this later in the essay. First, I'd like to provide a brief background to the moment the protests began in northern New Mexico.

On February 25, 2001, an exhibition titled "Cyber Arte: Where Tradition Meets Technology," opened in Santa Fe's International Museum of Folk Art where artist Alma Lopez was present to discuss her digital artwork, "Our Lady." A few weeks later, protests were set in motion. Letters and phone calls targeted the museum and New Mexico legislators, then, New Mexican Catholics held a rally and vigil to protest the image of a "bikini-clad virgin."

Archbishop Michael J. Sheehan, head of the Santa Fe archdiocese, made the following statements: "Here is the mother of God depicted like a tart or a call girl." He further called for the removal of the artwork claiming that a publicly supported museum had no right to display such a negative image of Mary.[62]

Just a short few weeks later on April 4th, the Museum of New Mexico board of regents held a forum to provide dissenters and supporters with a place to voice their concerns. Hundreds of protesters could not even enter the over-crowded meeting, obliging the regents to reschedule the forum for mid-April. In a larger meeting space, about one-hundred-and-fifty community members spoke, most of whom protested the "allegedly blasphemous" art by Lopez.[63]

To their credit folk-art museum Director Joyce Ice and Museum of New Mexico Director Tom Wilson did not succumb to pressure and did not remove "Our Lady" from the exhibit. They did however agree to end the display of "Cyber Arte" a few months sooner than they had planned originally. A few years later, the American Society for the Defense of Tradition, Family and Property (TFP), reporting about the protest, claimed success because "nearly one-thousand offended Catholics" and over "65,000 protest postcards from all over the nation" browbeat the Santa Fe International Museum of Folk Art for the eight-month duration of the exhibit.[64]

My own relationship to La Virgen de Guadalupe is not complex. Like Lopez, I am a Chicana lesbian who honors my mother and her plight within patriarchal institutions that dictate limitations for women. I think this specific understanding allows mothers and daughters to respect each other's methods of revering La Virgen. When my aunts and mother visit my home and see La Virgen de Guadalupe in various forms and shapes hanging on walls, sitting on windowsills and placed in crevices throughout the house, they express contentment. They do not question why La Virgen appears as a tattoo on the back of a Chicana with a "butch" haircut in Ester Hernández's serigraph, "La Ofrenda" that is put on view in the hallway. Nor do they remark upon the amorous embrace between La Sirena and La Virgen de Guadalupe in Alma Lopez's digital collage exhibited on my bathroom wall. I think they prefer to focus on the more traditional representations of La Virgen displayed on walls, windowsills. What I also sense is that they do not want to seem disrespectful of the less than traditional images in my home. But what I know about my family is that while the women are exceedingly Catholic, these same women have a sense of humor. Privately, I imagine one of them would have probably said of "Our Lady," "*Ay, pero qué chichona*," while another would have noted, "*Pero, qué bonitas flores*" without judging or imposing censorship. Of course, no one made such remarks. Not publically anyway.

In her scholarship, Ada María Isasi Díaz invites us to observe the difference between what Catholic Chicanas and Latinas might declare publicly and what they may say privately. Isasi Díaz argues that Latinas are subversive in subtle, constructive practices. "Hispanas/Latinas temporarily adapt and pretend, or do not think or feel the way they are "supposed to."[65] For the feminist liberation theologian, these women may not oppose dominant power structures successfully; however, they assert "quiet but effective forms of resistance."[66] In this case, I would contend that although women publically protested Lopez's digital representation of the Virgen by holding vigils and going to the Museum to call for the removal of the art, they did not persist and sustain their protests in the same manner that three specific Chicano male ideologues did. In other words, the women did not seem as invested in writing unending complaints as these three men. However, women came forward and wrote to Lopez calling her epithets like "disgraceful bitch"[67] and as the excerpt below shows, a New Mexican woman labeled the artist "*sinvergüenza*," meaning shameless.

> "I was moved to tears when I saw the digital photograph of Our Lady. The artist, if she is Catholic and Hispanic as well, seems to have lost all respect for our culture and most especially or what our culture holds in

highest esteem. I am sure she did not learn this at her mother's knee. SINVERGUENZA."[68]

This next protestor is not as harsh even if she does offer advice to the artist: "this isn't very nice for Catholics who praise Our Lady of Guadalupe. have a little more respect for our lady and for yourself."[69]

I found that no one woman arose as a persistent critic in the same way certain men performed dogged condemnation. While I am not arguing that the protests were split along clear-cut gender-lines, I am arguing that an explicit patriarchal, Chicano nationalist voice would not go away. It was as if these three men decided that they held the burden of policing and disciplining the artist—a Chicana lesbian—because her representation of La Virgen endangered the very survival of the Chicano nation. I would also add that according to the email written to Lopez from 2001 to 2008, many Chicanas and Chicanos as well as women and men from other ethnic and racial groups unswervingly defended the artist.

Why are these nationalist men so invested in policing women's bodies, women's desires and women's sexualities? In his book, *The History of Sexuality,* Michel Foucault puts forth his notion of the repressive hypothesis to demonstrate why those with power practice power within the realm of sexuality. As he explains, the issue is not whether one says yes or no to sex; the real question is who gets to speak about sex and "which institutions prompt people to speak about it" (Foucault, 1978, 11). Moreover, he posits that various social and legal institutions may object to "wayward or unproductive sexualities" but their purpose is to conflate pleasure and power. He warns of "(T)he pleasure that comes of exercising a power that questions, monitors, watches, spies, searches out, palpates, brings to light: and on the other hand, the pleasure that kindles at having to evade this power, flee from it, fool it, or travesty it" (Foucault, 1978, 45). The theorist compels us to rethink how repression operates to illuminate sexuality but as it does so, the alleged repression also performs "perpetual spirals of power and pleasure" (45). Ultimately, the repression itself creates the endless cycle of fixation with sex and sexuality. It's an interesting dance in which power and pleasure become incontestable, fused and ever-present.

In the same way, the male-centered ideologues took over the discursive protests and what transpired was a language of sex that reinforced rigid gender roles within heteronormative relationships. The nationalists made statements that smacked of misogyny and homophobia as they defended historical and ecclesiastical traditions. When women voiced disapproval, on the other hand, they expressed it once and went on with their lives. Yet these three men would not let up. Deeming themselves as either leaders or spokesmen for a singular Chicano nation, José Villegas Sr., Pedro Romero Sedeño and Ernesto Cienfuegos were probably the most vociferous dissenters on paper. The women may have publicly protested but they did not participate in the ongoing email complaints that lasted for years after the museum exhibit was over. Taking the artist to task for misrepresenting "our *Madre*," the dissenters each had their own agenda. Villegas, a native of New Mexico, was the first to declare objections in his letter to Lopez on March 17, 2001. Pedro Romero Sedeño, who adamantly pointed out that he held a Masters in Fine Art, challenged Lopez's art calling the piece anything but art. Lopez, who also holds a Masters in Fine Arts, engaged in a lively debate with Sedeño as she defended her stance and her right to her own artistic method and imagination. In 2004 when the city of Fullerton in southern California prepared to put on display "Our Lady," Cienfuegos come forward as the voice speaking for a singular Chicano nation while objecting to the "decadent" Chicana lesbian artist's digital print.

"Our Lady" as Mother-Seducer

"Freudian psychoanalysis grants women the power of seducing and of being seduced, being . . . sexed and desiring subjects."[70]

Before I deconstruct passages from the letters to artist Lopez, let me back up momentarily and offer my critique of La Malinche as "phallic" mother to the Chicano nation. Elsewhere, I argued for the construction of decolonial motherhood by way of Malintzin Tenepal, more popularly known as La Malinche. I argued that ideologues of the Chicano nation despised Malinche as the betrayer of her people and Cortes's whore. But for Chicanas, Malinche bore a new race. She is the all-powerful, phallic mother who is feared and despised by the heteronormative Chicano nation. La virgen, on the other hand, is forever "virginal" and must remain sexless, nurturing and always forgiving. The virgin-whore dichotomy continues to rear its head in contemporary society. The nation's phallogocentric discourse insists upon inflicting a dichotomy that authorizes patriarchal institutions so they may continue to have power over women, both real and imagined.

Chicano nationalist discourse constructs its own discursive trappings by reinforcing the good woman/bad woman binary. Women should not aspire to be Malinche, the whore but at the same time women can never be as holy and pure as La Virgin de Guadalupe. The challenge is that they must try to be. There are no in-betweens. No real women need apply since sexualized women are by definition already whores.

Examples of Male-Centered Discourse

> What is particular to modern societies, in fact, is not that they consigned sex to a shadow existence, but that they dedicated themselves to speaking of it *ad infinitum*, while exploiting it as the secret.[71]

Chicano activist and New Mexico resident José Villegas wrote a scathing letter of protest to artist Alma Lopez a few weeks after the exhibit with "Our Lady" opened in Santa Fe. I've included a few, revealing paragraphs from the email to demonstrate how Villegas himself is notably obsessed with "sacred images" of the Virgen and other Catholic icons. He is quick to point out that for him, Lopez has crossed "sacred boundaries" and disrespects over "five-hundred years of traditional values." Ironically, Villegas imposes a colonial mind-set that believes in customs that have been the weapons of colonization. He eagerly notes "the Immaculate Conception" to instruct the artist about religious tradition that she has overlooked.

March 17, 2001
Dear Ms. Lopez:

As you know or aware of [sic], our local Santa Fe newspaper wrote a story "Skimpily Attired 'Our Lady' Protested." So far, the community reaction to this story is very unfavorable towards your Cyber Arte exhibit and you may find yourself in some serious trouble with our *raza* in Northern New Mexico. . . .

Some people say it is alright to do your own *onda* in art expression, however, when you cross the sacred boundaries of our *gente* traditional values of over five hundred years, you cannot imposed and/or provoke thought on an issue that will inflame emotions against your own *gente*.

A point of clarification, Our Nuestra de Guadalupe picture really constitutes Guadalupe. It is taken as representing the Immaculate Conception. . . .

Our *Indio*-Chicano-Mexican religious beliefs, customs, traditions, principles and value system is part of an entire Nuestra de Guadalupe story. Our sacred images and religious symbols is the foundation of our faith and belief systems in place and should not be taken advantage of . . . Again, these sacred images belong to the indigenous people of the Americas, not you and/or your new-age ideology that your exhibit portrays as "Cyber-Arte Tradition Meets Technology."

Que Viva La Raza!
Que Viva La Causa!
Que Viva Los Brown Berets!
Que Viva César Estrada Chávez!

José L. Villegas, Sr.
Chicano Activist

Villegas uses Chicano nationalist libratory slogans to assure how much he himself believes in Chicano liberation. To write, "Que Viva La Raza," "Que Viva La Causa" and "Que Viva Los Brown Berets," the Chicano ideologue reconfirms a nation that practices colonial, heteronormative exclusionary acts by deciding who is and who is not a real Chicano or Chicana. In his mind, Lopez's feminist image opposes all things Chicano. And it is his anti-feminist vision of the nation that he inserts into gender roles.

When a supporter of Lopez challenged Villegas' anti-feminist and anti-lesbian stance, the critic defended himself:

At no time did I personally attack Alma because of her sexual orientation and/or gender due this type of art. And I will not even go there! *Órale!*

On a personal note, it was my mother's love that created the man that I am. It is my mother's *sangre* and tears that has mold me to what I am today. I have never disrespected my elders and their elders, especially *"la mujer"* in my barrio.[72]

Again, what is reaffirmed in the message above is the nationalist shift to place woman on a pedestal and as the good woman she is desexualized and reified as holy mother. For these nationalist men, you simply do not mess with their vision of the holy mother.

Artist Pedro Romero Sedeño wrote numerous emails to artist Lopez because he seemed convinced he had a lesson to teach her about "true" art. For Sedeño, Lopez's art was not art at all and his messages articulated a patronizing, patriarchal posture. At no time does he say that he respects Lopez, the artist. Instead he asserts that he, Pedro Romero, is the authentic artist and Lopez's art should never have been exhibited in any museum: "I reiterate here that Alma Lopez has every right to make whatever, and if this Museum wants to prop the notion that what she made is of artistic merit, I, Pedro Romero, have every right to question the merit of the 'work.'"[73]

In the paragraphs below, Sedeño, decides to offer his expertise as one who has rights to interpret La Virgen de Guadalupe. For him, Lopez's daring interpretation is culturally and historically wrong. Only he can really know the genuine cultural and historical meaning of "Our Lady." In Sedeño's mind, Lopez is neither artist nor intellectual therefore she is not entitled to her own historical rendering of famous female icons. But what I also find intriguing is Sedeño's personal attack against Lopez. He fears that Lopez believes women are unforgiving and retaliatory when in fact women should "bestow compassion." His revealing assertion proves how yet another Chicano nationalist ideologue insists that women must restrict themselves to specific gender roles and those roles call for ongoing forgiveness regardless of men's "sins."

Alma's concept of feminine strength is that of a woman ready to retaliate, not one prepared to bestow compassion. Depicted are princesses of destruction, not the Queen of Creation. . . . Alma Lopez's and her supporters' mistake is to claim that her piece is an interpretation of Guadalupe, a less valid one at that. The work is more about the myth of the ego of Alma Lopez , an ego that deceives her to believe "retaliate, don't forgive," an anti-myth made to stand up to the creation of compassion. This analysis can be applied also to the La Lupe series as a whole. Guadalupe does not

cavort with La Sirena, who does not exist, except in myths and
lotería cards and in the myth, in my opinion, that Alma Lopez actually cares about the feelings of respect or value a viewer may
have for Guadalupe-Tonantzin, our compassionate Mother.[74]

In a message sent a week earlier, Sedeño emphasized that
women are best represented in rigid gender roles. "I think feminist art comes into its full power when it acknowledges and up-
holds, rather than ignores, the maternal values of womanhood."[75]

Through May of 2002, Sedeño sustained his objections and
wrote more emails to illustrate how his was the correct conviction
while "a Chicano ideology that seeks to repudiate the image of
Our Lady of Guadalupe as a Catholic and European invention, a
"colonizing" instrument, as Alma Lopez puts it"[76] is erroneous.
Never mind scholarship that has shown the colonizing effects of
Christianity in the Americas.[77]

Other male critics who protested "Our Lady" wrote electronic
mail from 2001 to 2005, illustrating more male-centered discourse with a deep desire to discipline the female artist. For example, seventy-two year old Carlos Martinez, a resident of Santa
Fe, New Mexico, wrote that he was "extremely offended" by
Lopez's rendering of "the blessed Virgin Mary the mother of our
Savior Jesus Christ in a bikini" and that he was disappointed to
discover the artist is "Hispana" and therefore "should know better than to show utter disrespect" for the "Mother of the Americas."[78]

The following email from a Euro-American man was exceedingly offensive:

Dear Birdbrain,

You state that your intentions were not to offend the
Blessed Mother. Now tell me, in what state of mind (abnormal), could you justify degrading the most sacred
woman to ever grace this planet. Your feminist, twisted-

sisters don't care who they offend as long as there cause is carried forward [sic]. You not only insult our Mother, but her Son also, by portraying His Mother in such a vile manner."[79]

And another letter from yet another Euro-American man was equally as offensive:

This is blasphemy & deadly to your Soul.[80]

Note the manner in which "birdbrain," and "feminist twisted-sisters" are conflated in the first letter showing disdain for women as thinking, critical beings. The author proclaims that Lopez must know feminists are stupid and have no right to intellectual discourse. While Villegas and Sedeño spoke as the entitled, truthful Chicano voices hailing from New Mexico, Ernesto Cienfuegos anointed himself the Chicano voice of Aztlán in southern California.

Homophobia Is Aztlán

The letter by Ernesto Cienfuegos is perhaps the most disturbing since he authors a contemporary online newsletter/magazine that advertises spiteful misogyny and homophobia. Single-handedly, Cienfuegos attacks Lopez repeatedly focusing upon her sexuality and naming her and her work "sexually deviant." By "putting sex into language," Cienfuegos lays bare his own pervasive discourse about the "Guadalupe in a Bikini," "the lesbian artist," the "Sapphic pose," "the lesbian lover," "the sexually deviant lesbian connotations," "homosexual and lesbian lifestyles" as well as an editorial titled, "Chicana Lesbians Denigrate La Virgen" in another issue of his online journal.

Sample paragraphs from his letter represent Cienfuegos's disdain for Lopez.

To: Joe Felz, Director, Fullerton Museum Center, August 1, 2004

Dear Mr. Felz:

Our news publication, *La Voz de Aztlán*, has received your press release concerning the planned exhibit "The Virgin of Guadalupe: Interpreting Devotion" to open on August 28. Your press release mentions that as part of the exhibit, you will be including the highly offensive "Guadalupe in a Bikini" by the decadent lesbian artist Alma Lopez.

Sir, you may not be aware but the image has extremely sexually deviant symbolism and has already been condemned by millions of Mexicans here in the USA and in Mexico.

Firstly, the person in the sapphic pose representing the "Mother of Jesus" is nothing less than Raquel Salinas, the lesbian lover of the so called artist Alma Lopez. Raquel Salinas calls herself "La Chuparosa" which Alma Lopez often depicts on her abominable images. For a full description of the sexually deviant lesbian connotations of "Chuparosa" and of other symbolisms in Lopez' rendering of "La Reina de México," please read our editorial "Chicana Lesbians Denigrate La Virgen de Guadalupe" which can be read on our website on the Internet at http://aztlan.net/lupe.htm

Mr. Felz, we would like to think that you are merely ignorant of the facts and not involved in an anti-Mexican effort to destroy our most revered spiritual beliefs and cultural values. We would like to believe that the City of Fullerton's intentions for "The Virgin of Guadalupe: Interpreting Devotion" exhibit is to extend the hand of friendship to the large and growing Mexican population of Orange County and not to, like many anti-Mexicans xenophobes, to denigrate the values of our community in collusion with those in the homosexual and lesbian lifestyles and of those others who have a deep hate against us.

We are requesting that you refrain from exhibiting these and other offensive and abominable renderings of the Mexican "Holy Mother." Please, let us know before the City of Fullerton City Council's meeting of August 3 of your decision to refrain from destroying the faith based beliefs of the youths who attend Fullerton's educational system and of those others in our community.

Respectfully,
Ernesto Cienfuegos,
Editor-in-Chief, *La Voz de Aztlán.*

Cienfuegos was successful. His rhetorical turn alerted the Director of the Fullerton Museum Center who probably did not want the same kind of controversy in his museum that had already occurred in Santa Fe. The museum, however, did exhibit other artwork by Lopez.

Four years later in 2008, Cienfuegos continued to perpetuate alarming homophobia in his online journal, *La Voz de Aztlán.* Recently reporting the gay and lesbian protest marches in Los Angeles, CA where Proposition 8, the anti-gay marriage bill passed, *La Voz de Aztlán* reported, "It now appears that the issue of sodomite marriages may be headed back to the California Supreme Court."[81] The editor of the online news magazine further noted that a Black youth declared to the *Los Angeles Times*, "the so-called 'gays' are asking for major trouble" and a Latino youth remarked, "It may be time to send the homosexuals back into the closet."[82]

Remarkably, Cienfuegos is a self-appointed ideologue of the Chicano nation. Naming his online "news" mag-rag *La Voz de Aztlán* is an exceedingly arrogant declaration. He has led himself to believe his misogynist, homophobic voice, which is out of touch with multiple, diverse perspectives in the growing Chicano/a communities, is the voice of the Chicano nation. Yet, *La Voz de Aztlán* has been operating under his name for over a decade. While the online journal reports news and opinions about anti-Mexican immigration, Ku Klux Klan racism, biographical features on important Chicano/a leaders like César Chávez and Dolores Huerta, as well as think-pieces by Chicano professors Rudolfo Acuña and Armando Navarro, for the most part, the journal spouts an explicit patriarchal dogma that can be found in the criticism against artists like Alma Lopez. Cienfuegos himself has repeatedly criticized Chicana lesbians and I suspect he will continue to express his reactionary views so long as he publishes his online diary.

Pro-Arte

> Our Lady represents the inter-linkage of racial identities and sexual and political desires, while, at the same time, pointing to the constitutive ambivalence of the heart of Chicano/a—and other—identity formations.[83]

In her book, *Mujerista Theology*, Ada Maria Isasi-Díaz argues that community Catholic women are always reinscribing their own brand of Catholicism to fit their needs. Although the parish priests may not condone women's practices, the women perform their type of Catholicism despite male patriarchal objections.

Earlier I asked, how do we decolonize our community's perspectives about La Virgen de Guadalupe? What I have attempted throughout this essay is to show that the answer lies in decolonizing the minds of a community ruled by historical, colonial relationships that continue to stamp contemporary lives and culture. To decolonize the community, members of that kinship must intervene and test traditional rites that only serve to further colonize. By offering up her art, Lopez pushed the parameters of gender debates and compelled Santa Fe women and men to take a position about "Our Lady." When residents of New Mexico wrote to local newspapers, marched in protest and confronted each other, they began debates that forced them to reconsider women's traditional roles through representations of La Virgen. By writing emails to Lopez and engaging in a discussion, colonial mindsets were put into motion and challenged the very thing that has held women in traditional roles—a patriarchal Catholic Church. Lopez propelled the shift into decolonial mindsets when she put flesh on La Virgen de Guadalupe and freed "Our Lady" from the chains of patriarchal vision and expectations.

The following examples prove that there are those eager to transform for the betterment of the community rather than holding on to a colonial past that has only reinforced a virgin/whore dichotomy that has been detrimental to all women and all men.

"In our community images of La Virgin, San Judas Tadeo, even Jesús Cristo himself have been cultural icons for decades. I wonder if there exist 'less than appropriate' representations of these icons in gardens, stores, jewelry, clothing or even dishes in Santa Fe? I wouldn't be surprised. How would Mr. Villegas explain the usage in this case?"[84]

Another resident of New Mexico objected to Villegas in the following manner: "On your website, I read José Villegas' email to you, and I was sorry that he had the nerve to speak for all of Northern New Mexico."[85]

And then, a pointed criticism from another local woman demonstrated that not all New Mexicans agreed with Villegas. "I suspect that what is infuriating all these caballeros in Northern New Mexico is NOT the costume, but the loss of the all-loving, all-forgiving, all-nurturing mom."[86]

The quote from the following Chicano shows how there are men from the community who are willing to see another perspective. "The image of "Our Lady" forces me to take a second look at my own indoctrination where an exposed female body is seen as promiscuous and unholy.[87]

Finally, a daughter elucidates the life of her eighty-three-year-old New Mexican mother who spoke about her own mother's life in early twentieth century New Mexico and by doing so clarifies the value of Lopez's art. The quote is in the daughter's voice:

> She then proceeded to tell me what a feminist her own mother was working on the farm along the Rio Grande in NM. Gramma bought men's shoes so she could work outside, she wore Grampa's overalls and she cut her hair. She worked outside and raised 10 children inside. Mom said she was a modern thinker. Your piece keeps affecting people's lives and their thinking.[88]

Artist Alma Lopez's digital print, "Our Lady," represents a transformative move toward decolonization in which the virgin/whore binary is disrupted and women are honored for their multiple ways of being. Because the male ideologues could not see the work as art, they refused to acknowledge the intervention by a Chicana lesbian artist who compelled the Chicano nation to quit marking women as colonial objects. Through "Our Lady" Lopez declares, Chicanas and Latinas are subjects who live, love and desire. We refuse to be colonized any longer.

Decolonial Border Queers: Case Studies of Lesbians, Gay Men and Transgender Folks in El Paso/Juárez

". . . but I don't consider myself gay, not because I think, that 'ugh!' you know, it's because I see me and I see a gay male right here, and then I see [a] heterosexual male on the other side, you know what I mean, and I'm, like, in the middle . . ."
—Oral Interview with transgender, Coca Sapien, 2001, p. 14

How do queers in the US-Mexico cities of El Paso and Juárez "recognize themselves as subjects of a sexuality" and what "fields of knowledge and types of normativity have led Chicana/o lesbians, gay men and transgender folks to experience a particular subjectivity?[89] I want to consider this specific, historical, political border to argue that for these border queers of color, the particular fields of knowledge that make up their sexuality is an epistemology of coloniality. More importantly, queers in El Paso and Juárez, must engage and perform decolonial practices to survive the colonial landscape.

When I began my study of queer Chicanas/os and Mexicanas/os in a region that was my home for fourteen years, I realized that questions outnumbered answers and that the twenty-four transcripts of oral interviews in my possession would only provide cursory insights into the lives of a few lesbians, gay men, bisexuals and transgender folks in these geographic borderlands.[90] My friend and former colleague at the University of Texas in El

Paso, Gregory Ramos, conducted the oral interviews from 2000 to 2002 and subsequently wrote a poignant, performance piece, titled "Border Voices," inspired by the LGBT people he interviewed. Of the twenty-five interviewees, seven were women, seventeen were men and one was a transgender woman. Six of the seven women identified as Chicana, *fronteriza* or Hispanic. One was white. Of the men, twelve identified as Chicano, Hispanic or Mexicano; one was African American, one was Latino with parents from El Salvador, and three were white men.[91] Overall, the majority of interviewees identified as Chicana/o, Mexican or Hispanic. Those interviewed probably represent a cross-section of the predominantly Chicana/o and Mexican communities of El Paso where seventy-eight percent of the population is of Mexican origin. Although some of the Chicano/a interviewees may have been born in Juárez, or have family in Juárez, only one of the twenty-five said he was a Mexicano from Juárez. Although he lived in El Paso, his dual citizenship allowed his allegiance to Mexico.[92]

Making sense of wide-ranging realities for Chicana/o queers on the United States-Mexico border in the twenty-first century is not an easy task. I can only offer preliminary thoughts on a population of queers whose experiences are often neglected in more dominant discourses about queers in the US. I have constructed this introductory groundwork of border queers by borrowing from their words. The quotes here are from self-identified Chicana/o, Mexicana/o lesbians, gay men and transgender women and men. Of twenty-five interviewed, thirteen were Chicano or Mexican men who identified as gay or bisexual. Five were Chicanas who identified as lesbians although one of the women opted not to call herself a lesbian and declared more than once she was not gay although she had lived with her female partner for over fifteen years. Only one transgender Chicana/Mexicana told her story to Ramos and hers was a powerful, evocative story. I will not have an opportunity to quote from all of the interviews;

however, I have attempted to offer a glimpse into what it means to come out and live on the border as a queer of color, whether visibly out or not. From this cursory assessment, I argue that border queers are always already negotiating between a colonial burden and their decolonial practices.[93]

Before I can discuss the interviews, a concise historical background may clarify why I call the region a colonial space to be negotiated by those who live in these borderlands. To begin, the US-Mexico War of 1846-48 solidified a political border between two countries that could not agree where the geographic boundaries would divide its citizens. While the Nueces River in Texas had been the border between "Anglo" Texas and Mexico's state of Tejas y Chihuahua in 1836, United States President Polk pushed the boundary further south to instigate war with Mexico when he sent US troops to cross the Nueces River into Mexican territory. Shots were fired, a war was started and subsequently el Río Bravo, known on the US side as el Rio Grande became the recognized border.[94] But rivers shift and change, as do people, and the boundary may have been recognized politically but for those who had families on both sides of the Rio Grande, crossing did not stop from being a daily occurrence. Not until the immigration laws of the late nineteenth and early twentieth centuries did the crossing back and forth become a predicament for Mexican nationals living south of the border. Eithne Luibhéid claims that the Immigration Act of 1891 began the process of excluding immigrants "guilty of moral turpitude, that is, charges of adultery, bigamy, rape, sodomy," as well as anyone who exhibited "sexually abnormal behavior or appetites."[95] In her thought-provoking study, *Entry Denied,* Luibhéid introduces a case study of a Mexican lesbian in 1960 who was stopped at the border in Juárez for "looking like a lesbian," hence permitting the immigration officials to employ the Act of 1891.[96] The repercussions of this act and other immigration laws continue to affect the border communities, suggesting that even today, border queers decide carefully whether they will reveal their sexual identities.[97] At least half of those interviewed expressed that they may not live closeted lives but they remain discrete from fear of being ostracized. Immigration laws, when examined through a Foucauldian lens as a system of rules and constraints, reinforce racist and homophobic practices along the border and those practices, I argue, serve to silence queers of color who would ordinarily be far more open in a city not on the US-Mexico border. It becomes difficult for queers of color on the border to resist inequitable moral codes, which are not only imposed through laws and religion but also by way of hate crimes.

In other words, I'm stating that the policing and closing of the border meant securing a white colonial heteronormative way of seeing and knowing, hence fusing race with sexuality. As the Mexican Revolution of 1910 impelled many to flee north to the United States, the "Nativist" movement grew stronger and succeeded in passing quota acts in the early twentieth century favoring "Nativist" ancestors—white, Northern European immigrants. At the same time, eugenicists and sexologists worked hand in hand and as many looked south to Mexico, they imagined the impurities of a brown race threatening once again to overwhelm the white, pure race, perhaps even leading to miscegenation.[98] Sexual unions between brown and white had been dreaded since the US-Mexico War of 1846-48 and "Nativists" inherited that alarm.[99] Closing the border has been the solution to evading the raced, sexed body from Mexico.

Queers of color on the borderlands have inherited this thorny, colonial history. I have argued elsewhere that to decolonize history, a deconstructive method that I call the decolonial imaginary may be taken up. It is an interstitial space in which political and social dilemmas are negotiated and deconstructed. It is space in which one is not merely oppressed or victimized; nor is one only oppressor or victimizer. Rather, one negotiates between and among one's identities in favor of the identity that is most viable for that political, historical moment. The ongoing process of the negotiation itself must be understood as that—a process. In other words, the decolonial is a dynamic space in which subjects are actively decolonizing their lives. Unlike the colonial imaginary, which is a narrow, binary "us" versus "them" standpoint, the decolonial imaginary instead is a liberatory, mobile frame of mind. The decolonial is a deconstructive tool. It seeks out and challenges that which is written in history to write an alternative story. It seeks to unravel colonial, binary relations that we have inherited through historical circumstance such as wars and invasions.[100]

These oral histories are alternative stories even if the stories do not seem so different from emblematic coming out stories. Border queers are not vastly different from queers throughout the US who navigate daily struggles and contradictions. Lesbians, gay men, bisexuals and transgender folks continue to challenge discriminatory laws and social conventions globally but some geographic spaces are safer than others. In the United States, for example, LGBT populations flock to urban areas like New York City, San Francisco, Los Angeles and Chicago where many can live in clusters. Unfortunately, urban queers still face hate crimes and bigotry in these cosmopolitan cities, but often, a large population of queers may draw together to fight against discriminatory practices. On the border, where many queers of color prefer to be discrete, confronting homophobia is complex. Border queers face a delicate existence given the political, historical and socioeconomic challenges on the U.S-Mexico border. The interviews show how LGBT Chicanas/os are creative, forgiving and eager for social change even if the changes are only for "liberal" gay rights.

Chicana lesbian feminist and border theorist, Gloria Anzaldúa reminded us that to live on the border, one is both scapegoat and forerunner of a new race, one is man and women but also neither. In the borderlands, whether physical or metaphoric, queer experience is somewhere in the middle, somewhere in that interstitial space that I call the decolonial imaginary, between the colonial and the postcolonial. And somewhere "in the middle," to quote transgender Chicana/Mexicana, Coca Sapien, are the many genders that we have yet to recognize or name. Perhaps an investigation into these geographic borderlands, in which dualities of experience are common, can help us further understand global and transnational queer experiences.

I also claim that queers on the border experience their sexuality through a political economy founded on a colonial history and as a result border queers must navigate decolonial ways of being and knowing. The laws and discourses emerging from this colonial history pose specific contradictions for queers of color. Foucault has shown us the importance of examining the *production* of sexuality rather than it's *origins* and embedded in that style of investigation, was his concern for other kinds of oppressive conditioning. Like racism. If one turns to his lectures presented at the College of France from 1975-76, published posthumously, 1997 in France and 2003 in the United States, one sees Foucault pursuing not only the production of history, but also, he considers that which he has been accused of ignoring— race and discourse of racism. When he argued that history produces processes, whether the process is the language of sex and how sex is "put into language" or whether the process is war and how racism became the discourse of war, he was concerned with power, the power that creates that knowledge and the relations of power and knowledge that have come to be in the present (Foucault, *Society Must be Defended* 70). As I read his lectures, I realized that those of us who turn to Foucault's methodology have not been wrong to link race to sexuality. The persistent production of race, as it is linked to sex, is crucial. When we scrutinize racialized sexualities, then we must also peer closely at the persistent production of colonial relations to decide how colonial relations are often raced and sexed. When Foucault pointed out that "history is an operation of power, an intensifier of power," he acknowledged that the manner in which history is remembered or erased creates those who will be considered the lasting ideologues of an era.[101] He is, in fact, referring to the hegemonic, colonial stories that will be imparted through the decades and then through the centuries to construct a common understanding of our past.

This study then, is an initial look at the production of racialized sexualities and the manner in which queers of color have survived and negotiated their identities on the US-Mexico border, where the nation-state is as dubious as it is rigidly patriotic.

Negotiating Colonial/Decolonial Spaces

On the 1st of May 2002 I sat in my kitchen in El Paso, Texas, drinking my morning cup of coffee and, as I perused the *El Paso Times*, the headline seized my attention: "Victim of Hate Crime led 2 Lives, Friends Say." A photograph of a transgender Chicana accompanied the story. Héctor Arturo "Arlene" Díaz had been shot in the back and left to die on Anapra Road not far from a convenience store. The story read, "At home in Sunland Park, he was the baby boy of a hard-working mother, the sibling of nine brothers and sisters. At night, the 28-year-old man dressed in women's clothing and became 'Arlene,' a fixture of the gay scene in Downtown El Paso."[102] The murder had occurred on April 10th, a few weeks before I read the story about "Arlene." In fact, the newspaper on April 11th only reported that a man had been found dead in Sunland Park. There was no mention of a possible hate crime until further into the article. It's no wonder I hadn't read it. But the report of May 1st stunned me. By the time the police arrested the alleged killer on April 22nd, they classified Díaz's murder as a hate crime quite possibly motivated by "Díaz's sexual orientation."

The murder of "Arlene," a transgender Chicana, shook the LGBT communities in El Paso but queers on the border were not unfamiliar with hate crimes and gay bashing. In 1998, LAMBDA Community Service Center reported a fifty-three percent increase in assaults against queers while the police department claimed that there were almost no hate crimes in El Paso. LAMBDA, which opened its doors in El Paso in 1991, pointed out that victims of anti-gay hate crimes do not report to the police but do report to LAMBDA. "In 1997, the police documented only two incidents out of a total of eleven crimes motivated by prejudice. And 42 percent of the people reporting crimes to LAMBDA never called the police."[103]

Unfortunately, Arlene Diaz's murder did not garner national attention, not in the same way Brandon Teena's or Mathew Shepherd's brutal murders alerted us to the severity of anti-queer hate crimes in the United States. But the "historical emergencies" that occur on the border of US and Mexico often do not receive much notice.[104] Since 1993, hundreds, or perhaps closer to one-thousand, women in Juárez have been murdered or have been reported missing. While the murders and disappearances occasionally receive media attention beyond the region, those who live on the border cannot ignore the crisis. When I read about one more murder, one more hate crime, I was distraught but also recognized that even if the murderer was found guilty, social and moral codes on the border would continue to attempt to frighten queers of color into silence, hence into a colonial regime.

I do not want to characterize border queers as victims; they are anything but passive victims. Queers of color survive, resist and create defiant measures to change attitudes, rules and social codes on the border. For many, the border is a zone of tolerance, *una zona de tolerancia,* that serves to contain illicit, unwanted behaviors within specific spaces.[105] I argue that coming out on the border is a negotiation of a colonial space, compelling those who live out loud to become decolonial in their actions. Conceptually, a term like tolerance conveys a colonial perspective. Tolerance, after all, affirms the hierarchical ideology imposed from above by those who judge themselves as the only real, worthy citizens while those being tolerated are less than worthy. But what happens when we question how decolonial agency plays out for each queer of color who chooses to come out on the border especially as queers become more and more direct, outspoken and active. Realistically, when queers break out and away from safe zones of colonial tolerance in which they are contained to protect a heteronormative society, queers then face harsh criticism, hostility and hate crimes. It is outside of the zones of colonized tolerance that queers practice their decolonial political activity. But I seem to be making value judgments. I do not assume that within those colonial zones, border queers do not also practice subtle resistances. Anybody who lives in the margins knows that daily life is a decolonial practice in which one must negotiate various power structures to survive. I'm merely pointing out that when border lesbians, gay men and transgender folks break out of the spaces in which they are contained, whether those spaces are designated "bars" or homes, so that they do not contaminate a pure, heteronormative society, that the breaking out itself is an act of defiance that surpasses any imposed notions of tolerance. In this way, queers of color on the border become decolonial performers.

"I'm Here, a Brown Queer!"

An archetypal, progress narrative surfaced as queers of color from El Paso and Juárez told their stories eager to share openly their identities as queer Chicanas/os and Mexicans. The older gay men and lesbians, who came out as early as the 1950s, had harsh stories to tell about their lives on the border while a younger generation expressed a rebelliousness made possible from the LGBT rights fought for after the 1970s.

One of the oldest of the gay men interviewed, Manuel Madrid, was seventy years old at the time of his interview in 2002. Manny was born in San Elizario, Texas, a small town outside of El Paso, and his parents moved to the city when he was nine years old. Although he could not speak English, he learned the language swiftly in a grade school with a majority of English-speaking non-Mexicans. When his parents separated, he was left with his grandmother who raised the young boy (Madrid 7). By the time Manny reached high school, probably as early as 1948, he identified his sexual feelings for boys and decided to confess his yearning to a priest. When the priest told him he was committing a sin, Manny decided resolutely never to speak again to a Catholic cleric about his same-sex desire. Unlike other devout Catholics who were interviewed, Manny escaped guilt and did not brand himself a sinner. Instead, he and his best friend in high school would single out boys to each other, commonly referring to them as "joto," and concluding "I think he's with us" (Madrid 13, 18-19). He asserted that he did not come out in El Paso because in the 1950s most queers were closeted and as far as he knew there was only one bar in town that accepted a gay clientele. He would, however, pick up Fort Bliss soldiers and have sex with them in the desert. Manny said he finally came out in 1966 when he moved to Los Angeles, where he lived with his partner, Marshall, of twenty-two years but after he died of colon cancer, Manny returned to El Paso (Madrid 24). "I could kick my butt for moving back to El Paso," he said (Madrid 44). Grieving for his partner those first few years were difficult but after eight years back on the border, Manny concluded "El Paso is beautiful and a healthier place to live than LA" (Madrid 34).

The only family member that Manny came out to was his niece—a lesbian and despite his aunt having lived in the same house with Manny and his partner, Manny did not tell her he was gay. "I think our sexuality is nobody's business but our own," he added.[106]

Similarly, Armando, a self-identified bisexual, was forty-seven at the time of his interview. He asserted, "The gay community is very much, I guess, reflective of me, of how I am . . . pretty much everybody's in hiding" (Armando 8). Unlike Manny, Armando stayed in El Paso and fell in love with an older married man with children. The married man, who claimed to be "Christian," left Armando broken-hearted. The experience, however, gave him the courage to face his sexuality despite choosing a closeted life.[107]

By contrast, Yolanda Leyva, forty-five, made a point to be out at the age of eighteen when she began to go to queer bars in El Paso. A Chicana lesbian, who is currently a professor of History at the University of Texas in El Paso, Yolanda was born in Juárez and grew up in El Paso where she came out in the 1970s. Going to bars "made me really aware of how dangerous it was to be a gay person in El Paso" in the 1970s, she said (Leyva 7). In other words, harassment was common. Queers had to cope with the police who would go into the bars, order the lights turned on and then file the clientele into the parking lot to check their identification. To add to that harassment, patrons entering and leaving the bar endured persecution from drunk, seemingly heterosexual men who lingered in the parking lot with the sole purpose of bullying regulars (Leyva 8).

The harassment did not stop Yolanda from patronizing bars or other queer spaces. She would even cross-dress sometimes and her mother would help her dress in men's suits declaring, "Mija, you look so handsome, the women are really gonna love you" (Leyva 8). However, when her sixty-year-old mother realized that Yolanda was actually dating women, they had an argument and her mother called her a "*jota*" (Leyva 11).

Shortly after their argument, Yolanda moved to Austin where she became active with lesbian groups. After living in Austin, Tucson and San Antonio, she returned to her home in El Paso. Although she had other job opportunities, she chose El Paso because for her, the border is a unique space where its inhabitants can explore multiple identities created by the many cultures in the region.

For Yolanda, growing up gay in a Chicano family is different from "mainstream" America: "I think a lot of people have this stereotype that it's harder to be gay in a Chicano family and part of that is because of Catholicism and because Chicanos are seen as more conservative socially. But what I've seen . . . is that because Chicanos put such emphasis on family, that I've seen a lot of gay men and lesbians really accepted by their families, even though the families don't like that their children are queer, I've seen a lot of acceptance."[108]

It's an interesting double-turn of colonial imposition and decolonial practice for those coming out on the border. While on the one hand, Armando and Manny were for the most part closeted; there were family members, as in Manny's case, who more or less accepted the queer in the family so long as the secret was not discussed or flaunted. In other words, Chicana/o lesbians and gay men are expected to keep silent and remain loyal to the patriarchal familial oppression that is convenient for their/our families. Even while practicing the decolonial, radical politics of "I'm here, a brown queer," Chicanas/os are asked to abide by "don't ask, don't tell" homophobic diplomacy that erases our very existence.[109] However, many still defy homophobic colonial tolerance and choose to speak out and perform their decolonial agency. Hence, many queers renegotiate their place in the family and as Leyva pointed out, Chicana/o families may not like that they have a queer daughter or son but the acceptance occurs more often than not. At the same time, however, the acceptance still transpires within a patriarchal familial structure that queers are obligated to mediate.

Jorge Garcia, also known as Sasha, felt compelled to leave his home in El Paso before he could come out. At nineteen years old he lived in San Angelo, Texas where he was attending technical school in 1988. He walked into a gay bar in San Angelo and experienced a gratifying homosexual encounter, the second of his life. The first had occurred when he was a thirteen-year-old high school student. Jorge said he was sexually assaulted by a "jock," who had persistently hassled him. In the urinal one day, Jorge realized the jock had always wanted to have sex with him and asked him to "suck" his dick. Frightened and excited, the young men walked to the desert where they could be alone and the "jock" proceeded to assault Jorge (García 6). "I kept telling him to stop and he wouldn't . . . I was on the floor, on the ground, the dirt, on my stomach and he was on top of me. And he wouldn't stop" (García 13-15). The "jock" finally released Jorge, who got up, put on his pants and walked home silently.

When he was older, Jorge moved to Dallas and was content with the queer communities he encountered but after a breakup with a lover, Jorge returned to El Paso in 1993 to attend the University of Texas in El Paso. Because he felt stifled, he spent summers in California where he was "taken aback" by Gay Pride in San Francisco (García, 17-18, 20, 25-6). Having performed "drag" in his early twenties in San Angelo and in Dallas, Jorge decided to perform again when he impersonated Lorena Bobbit in a Halloween skit. Around 1998, he told his mother and sister about his drag performances and they encouraged him to continue. At the gay bar the Old Plantation (O.P.), he would impersonate Linda Ronstadt and sing from her album, "Canciones de mi Padre" or he would mimic Eartha Kitt. Pageants became important to Jorge who by now was known more by his drag name, Sasha. Sasha, who came out at nineteen, claimed that life for queers in El Paso had improved so much since his high school experience that in 2001 he could sit in a Denny's coffee shop with his queer friends, each of them dressed in drag, and not be harassed.[110]

Pepe Porras, a gay Mexicano, born in El Paso but raised in Mexico grew up with the privilege of country clubs and boarding schools. He was kicked out of his house in Juárez where he lived with his family when his father discovered Pepe naked in bed with a man. His father, while screaming *maricón*, ordered him to leave. Humiliated yet relieved that his family finally knew he was gay, Pepe left his home and returned the next day for his clothes and other personal items. His parents had already burned his possessions and painted his bedroom. The thirty-six year old left Juárez, took his first job and found an apartment in El Paso. Pepe said that his father grieved for months that his son was gay only acknowledging him by offering Pepe a monthly allowance with the condition that his father would never have to see his son again.[111]

Pepe, along with other gay men and lesbians interviewed, discussed machismo in Mexican culture, which served to reinforce roles among some queers. For example, Pepe confessed that when he was sixteen and initially experimenting with other men, he "was afraid to engage in penetration for fear he'd wake up feeling like a woman" (Porras 4). Now that he's older, he claims that he has no problem being gay because he's not identified as a gay man, whether in Mexico City, San Francisco or New York City. He prefers not to flaunt his lifestyle and states that queers who are too open are the cause of violence against them. He concluded: "I don't see color, I don't see sexuality, I'm just me" (Porras 8).

Although Pepe and Armando are from different generations, they seem to share similar judgments that reinforce sexual hierarchy among gay men. "In Mexico, if you're the top, then you're the male, hence not gay. But if you're on the receiving end, then you're the gay one. In Juárez, lots of married men have sex with other men."[112]

Myrna Avalos, a Chicana lesbian, also commented on machismo. She believes that the border city breeds *machista* attitudes toward women, which take the form of drunkenness, womanizing and battering. She was very critical of this "cultural thing" (Avalos 1). For Myrna, butch women in lesbian bars exhibit territorial behavior that she did not like. She said she would go to You Got It, a lesbian bar that had to close down around 1996 because the police had to break up fights between lesbians too often. "I mean these women would literally fight. Throw bottles at each other. I mean, territorial . . . with their women. 'This is my woman, you leave her alone, Bop!'" (Avalos 24). She named their territorial behavior a "butch pussy-stance" and refused to engage in the type of restrictive role-playing that was anti-feminist. Identifying as a butch lesbian for Myrna meant negotiating role-playing within a patriarchal structure that already condemned women. She adamantly reclaimed her butch identity as a role beyond "*machista*" behavior that was confining to women, particularly lesbians (Avalos 4, 11).

Myrna came out in El Paso at the age of seventeen and although she is out and works at a gay bar, before then, she put up with six brothers, their homophobic remarks and an extended family asking her when she planned to marry (Avalos 14-15). The Old Plantation (a problematic colonial name) is one of the longest standing gay bars in El Paso, having opened in the early 1970s. Myrna noted that it was once taboo to mention the O.P. but around the mid-1990s, heterosexuals began to go to the club (Avalos 17-18, 21). In fact, almost all of the queers interviewed mention that the O.P. has become increasingly "straight" and that queers do not to go on Saturday nights when heterosexuals swarm the space. Myrna attests that presently (in 2002) she has seen police officers and lawyers, both gay and straight at the bar but in and around 1994-95, it was customary for homophobic straight clientele to go to the queer bar expressly to beat up gays and lesbians. Subsequently, a sign has been placed on the wall that announces, "This business is gay owned and gay operated" and Myrna also claims that gays no longer put up with the bashing in their own queer space. Most accept that queers will be the majority on Friday nights. She claims that gay men and lesbians have stopped going on Saturdays when so many heterosexuals overrun the bar. What Myrna also noted was the stigma about being an out gay person. When she saw clients in the other spaces of the city, they ignored her for fear that she would recognize them as customers of the O.P. (Avalos, 17-18, 21). In a sense Myrna attributes the less than open queer community with the fact that there is no authentic lesbian group or organization in El Paso to meet their needs. She also blames what she has coined, "pussy-stance mentality," for hindering lesbians from activism that would confront homophobia. Instead, lesbians are too busy fighting over their "women," but she also accuses a conservative population in Texas of severe homophobia that impedes successful organizing in El Paso (Avalos 26).

Twenty-one year old David Andrew Rubalcava identifies as a Hispanic American gay male. He was born and raised in El Paso and was a student at UTEP during the time of the interview. His queer play, "A Piece of Mind," was staged in El Paso at the LAMBDA Center to a supportive El Paso audience. David has supportive, loving parents, siblings and friends. He believes that people in the border region have close-minded attitudes toward gays. David enjoys dispelling stereotypes by coming out to as many people as he can. For him, education will transform the border into a more egalitarian place compelling the population to eradicate homophobia. David expressed that coming out and living an openly gay life gives him the opportunity to educate heterosexuals who hold stereotypes of queers. As a young man, he is unyielding about his rights as a gay man. When asked about Catholicism, he remarked, "Fuck that, I'm not gonna listen to this bullshit because who are they to say who I can fall in love with, who I can have sex with, what kind of sex I can have, if I can use birth control or not, if I can make decisions about my own body."[113]

Decolonial Performers

After reviewing the voices in these interviews, I infer that by living their lives in what could be considered a decolonial critical stance, queers of color assert an oppositional posture at the same time that they must negotiate between what has been inherited—a history of racism, homophobia, coloniality—and what is being contested and decolonized—racism, homophobia, coloniality—and what is hoped for—an end to racism, homophobia, coloniality, hence there is a subtle move toward the postcolonial ideal which remains an impossible dream for US Chicanas/os. What is possible, however, is a decolonial way of being and knowing on the US-Mexico border where Chicana/o and Mexican lesbians, transgender folks and gay men negotiate their lives as "out" citizens with third class rights (Avalos 30-31).

Queer theorist, José Muñoz argues that "the politicized agent must have the ability to adapt and shift as quickly as power does within discourse."[114] We must assume the agent is politicized in ways that will permit a decolonial queer method but even if not politicized, border queers of color are creative daily as they negotiate dignity and survival. Having lived in El Paso for ten years and in Juárez for one year in the 1990s, I witnessed and experienced the manner in which homophobia pressed down against the queer of color population but I also saw Chicana/o queers constructing full lives while being cognizant that living on the border is its own political challenge. Queers on the border do not and cannot forget the poverty and racism that infects the region. Myrna speaks as a politicized agent who is not only eager to decolonize the border but knows that change is absolutely necessary for survival on the border. She states in the following quote:

> We need to fight . . . we've lost our humanity. I'm not just speaking about El Paso . . . we have the border right here, we see cardboard boxes, homes. That's their home. . . . We talk about 'world poverty' and 'world hunger' when I can just turn around and see, see the reality. And people just read it in books . . . here especially too, they read, 'oh, there's world hunger?' Just look

across the border, just look. . . . I think we should fight for
humanity a little more, especially here in El Paso.[115]

David, one of the youngest of those interviewed, embraces
his gay life and by doing so he is defying the homophobia still
present in the borderlands. Sasha, also of a younger generation,
learned to defy the assaults he had experienced as a younger man
in El Paso by choosing to be out as a queer performer. Yolanda,
an out Chicana lesbian and scholar-activist born in the 1950s,
consistently challenges the status quo and fights for social justice in El Paso. The older generation, like Manny and Armando,
still manage to live gratifying queer lives despite the severity of
homophobia they experienced.

El Paso and Juárez queers negotiate a severely racist and heteronormative colonial space that attempts to negate their lived
experiences. Anyone living in the borderlands knows that, but to
be a queer of color *en la frontera* also means the task is that much
trickier. "Arlene" Díaz, the transgender Chicana who was murdered by an enraged transphobic man represents the overarching
sense of despair in a region that continues to see violence inherited from a history of coloniality. Queers who live in El Paso and
Juárez must perform decolonial practices to survive the colonial
landscape in a space where "people walk through you, the wind
steals your voice, you're a burra, buey, scapegoat, forerunner of
a new race, half and half—both woman and man, neither—a new
gender . . ."[116]

So Far from God, So Close to the United States: A Call for Action by US Authorities

Poor brown women are being murdered in the border city of Juárez, Mexico. Since 1993, the families and friends of victims have been painting black crosses with pink backgrounds on telephone poles throughout the city to remind those who pass that the deaths of an estimated 325 women and girls will not be ignored. Another 400 to 450 women and girls have "disappeared" in the last nine years. In a city with a population of 1.2 million, how can nearly 800 murders and disappearances go unsolved without any convictions? (And this says nothing of the more than 1,000 men who have been murdered, probably because of links to the drug cartel.) Instead the murders have become part of the terrain, and although the victims' families have been crying for help for nearly a decade, still nothing has been done. That is, nothing has stopped the homicides in which women have been found brutally raped, some with breasts cut off, nipples bitten off and even organs ripped out.

More than 300 women's groups made up of families and friends of the victims have demanded justice since the homicides began. These grassroots groups originated in Juárez and have since spread to Chihuahua City and Mexico City, and to El Paso, Texas and Las Cruces, New Mexico. They are now spilling out beyond Mexico and the US border cities into the greater United

States, where many people, if they are even aware of the murders, assume that "it's their problem, not ours."

It is as if the lives of poor Mexican women are pennies in the big corporate machine of the maquiladora industry. The families of the victims are poor and powerless, so city officials see no need for the state or federal government to be concerned. None of these poor Mexican women were their daughters, sisters, wives or friends. President Vicente Fox has declared that his office will support investigations, but so far his help is only lip service. The former mayor of Juárez concluded that the slain women dressed provocatively and should have been at home instead of out on the street at night. The victims are therefore to blame in the eyes of city officials, who turn their backs on the citizens of their city. Many observers have accused the police and local government of such severe corruption that the murderers will go free as long as the investigation remains in the hands of the city government. Witnesses can point to police who have raped women, covered up evidence, conducted sloppy investigations and threatened anyone who is willing to come forward with information leading to the arrests of those responsible for the murders.

Across town from the city "fathers" of Juárez, the maquiladora industry, which hires many of the young women who end up dead, is thriving. It has no need to be concerned with a shortage of labor: a steady stream of young women continues to enter Juárez from rural areas to replenish the labor pool and take the places of the dead and missing. There are more than 200 maquilas in Juárez, many of which opened their doors when the North American Free Trade Agreement (NAFTA) was signed between the United States and Mexico in 1993, coincidentally the same year the murders started. Many of the women murdered were traveling home late at night from work, often at the maquilas, in city buses. The ride can take two to three hours; then the women must walk through deserted roads with no streetlights to guide their way. In fact, the maquilas make no effort to provide safe transportation for their employees despite attacks against women going to and from work. Many people have surmised that a particular clause of NAFTA precludes the Mexican government from holding the maquilas responsible in any way. The chapter 11 provision of the NAFTA agreement allows US companies to sue the Mexican government for any monetary losses, which include both actual profits and anticipated profits, incurred on account of protective environmental laws, labor laws or labor strikes. US companies may pollute the environment in Mexico and they may treat workers as disdainfully as they please, without retribution from Mexico. In the meantime, we in the United States can purchase inexpensive computers, cell phones, toys and other products made in Mexico by women who have turned up dead.

Conspiracies are alleged in which the wealthy and powerful are protected and hence untouchable. There is certainly no lack of conjecture. Fingers have pointed to international wealthy owners of maquilas and their sons, called "juniors," who need playmates with whom they can play "rough." Fingers also point to the drug cartel, which protects itself by threatening anyone who knows too much. Some claim that women are brutalized and murdered during the making of snuff films. Others charge that the women are murdered for organs that are sold on the black market. Still others contend that satanic cults that kill for the thrill perform the ritual murders. Some maintain that the serial killer or killers are from the United States and can cross the border easily, carry out murders in Mexico, then return to safe haven in their own country.

Is there a solution? We can throw up our hands and say, well, that's Mexico. Or we can throw money at the problem; the victims' families and the only rape crisis center in the city, Casa Amiga, will be grateful. But our response must go beyond writing checks and hosting fundraisers. We must alert the world that violations of human rights are occurring in our own back yard. The United States prides itself on its belief in democratic principles, in notions of free trade and in equal rights for women (in Afghanistan, anyway). But this is what free trade has brought to our door. If the US and Mexican governments can make trade agreements, why can't they also agree to solve and stop the murders of hundreds of Mexican women?

The Coalition against Violence toward Women and Families on the Border, based in El Paso, Texas, is making a number of demands. One calls for US government officials to begin immediate negotiations with Mexico to form a federal binational task force that could investigate the murders and bring justice to the murdered women's families. The Coalition also demands that US forensic scientists and laboratories be made available to Mexican investigators to identify and prosecute the criminals. So far, Juárez officials have refused assistance from the FBI, declaring that this is their problem and they do not want the Americans meddling. Precisely because it believes that local police are botching the investigations, and more than likely protecting the guilty, the Coalition contends that only a binational federal task force can help solve the murders.

But the US government will not intervene unless there is substantial pressure from the US public. As a result, the Coalition has recently proposed a letter writing campaign in which citizens throughout the United States would write letters to their lawmakers in Congress, demanding a federal binational task force with Mexico to investigate the murders. The sample letter below can serve as a model for a letter in your own words; use it and distribute it to your friends. You may also wish to phone in your message: the US Capitol switchboard at (202) 225-3121 can connect you with any congressional office in Washington, or you can phone your elected official's local office. The more we pressure our government to intervene in this international human rights scandal, the better the chances of stopping the murders and bringing justice to the victims' families.

Honorable [your Senator's name]
US Senate Washington, DC 20510
Or
Honorable [your Representative's name]
US House of Representatives Washington, DC 20515

Dear_____

I am appalled that more than 325 women have been murdered in Ciudad Juárez, Chihuahua, Mexico, since 1993 and an additional 400 women are missing. The killings and disappearances continue to this date. Almost a third of these women worked in maquiladora factories, many of them owned by companies based in the United States. Six of the women were US citizens. Some experts, including former FBI profiler Robert Ressler, believe that the murderers are serial killers from both sides of the US-Mexico border.

I respectfully request:

1. That US government officials begin immediate negotiations with government officials in Mexico to form a binational task force to investigate these crimes.
2. That US forensic scientists and laboratories be made available to investigators in Ciudad Juárez in a concerted effort to identify and prosecute the criminals.
3. That US-based firms that employ women in the maquiladoras be required to accept responsibility for the safety of their employees. Safe working conditions and safe transportation to and from employees' homes are needed.

4. That you create a fund that will provide a reward to informants who offer information leading to the arrest of perpetrators.

Hundreds of women in Mexico have been raped, tortured and murdered in the last decade. Mexican officials have been unable to stop these brutalities. We must not allow the utter disdain for the lives of Mexican women to continue.

Sincerely,

(Signature)

THE DECOLONIAL
IMAGINARY REVISITED

The Imaginary as Will to Feel: Beyond the Decolonial Turn in Chicanx/Latinx Feminism

> Because I do not wish to get caught up in complicated definitions, I propose to denominate as desire all forms of the will to live, the will to create, the will to love, the will to invent another society, another perception of the world, and other value systems.
>
> —Felix Guattari, *Molecular Revolution in Brazil*

> . . . feeling pleasures so much larger than skin and bones and blood.
>
> —Louise Erdrich, *Love Medicine*

I've been rethinking the decolonial as theory and method and I'd like to reassert that without the imaginary, the decolonial as theory becomes either universalist or essentialist in its impetus to clarify history and the present imprinted by history. In other words, we are prone to generalize too much, making sweeping arguments about "all Spanish as colonizers" and "all people of color as colonized" and hence erasing agency. As method, the decolonial has become a deconstructive tool that identifies European historical moments of conquest that usurped the land of Indigenous people in the Americas. The works of the usual suspects—Walter Mignolo (2002, 2007), Aníbal Quijano (2007), Nelson Maldonado-Torres (2007), Sylvia Wynter (2003) and others—speak to this extensively. Works that address feminism and

gender include those by Macarena Gómez-Barris (2017), María
Lugones (2006) and Chandra Mohanty (1988), as well as by Chicanx feminists Gloria Anzaldúa (2016), Chela Sandoval (2000),
Laura Pérez (2019), Dolores Delgado Bernal (2001) and Mariana
Ortega (2017), for example. And while my list is hardly exhaus-
tive, I think we can agree that the various schools of thought
and method that have emerged since the late 1990s usually stay
within the boundaries of their own critiques to ask questions
about the coloniality of power (Quijano), coloniality of knowledge (Mignolo), coloniality of being (Maldonado-Torres), coloniality of gender (Lugones) and decoloniality of *cuirs* (queers)
(Gómez-Barris).[117]

Where do these critiques and analyses take us? Chicanx/Lat-
inx and Indigenous feminists have been writing the decolonial in
ways not often recognized, while processing how the decolonial
as method may offer up new ways of knowing and being. These
epistemological and ontological perspectives have inculcated
Chicanx/Latinx and Indigenous feminisms.[118]

I'm asking, where are we now? Are we satisfied with the decolonial as method? As a deconstructive tool, does the decolonial necessarily expose colonial powers, structures, laws and
institutions? Is gender necessarily colonial? What are the flaws of
a decolonial theory that regards a materialist perspective while
occluding the spirit of the mind and body? It is as if the method
and the theory exist in parallel universes, never to touch or entice
each other but instead battling in a false binary. And yet we cannot have theory without method; we cannot have a materialist,
grounded "real" critique without the affective body, without the
people who feel, who touch, who experience and imagine other
ways of being. The imagination, after all, is the door to creativity, to other ways of being and knowing. Overall, the real without the imaginary lacks vision and affirms a two-dimensional,
uninspired ontology and epistemology.[119]

Elsewhere, I attempted to meld in word and argument what is already fused in body and mind: the decolonial and the imaginary. The various ways of conceptualizing decolonial methods and theories, when historically grounded in space and time, are already materialist. Materialist methods and theories cannot and should not be negated. Without regional and historical specificity, we tend to make broad, generalized statements about decolonial theories, relying too much on master narratives such as the Spanish conquest. While that historical era persistently marks our daily lives, whether we identify as Chicanx, Latinx, Indigenous, Asian Latinos, or Black Latinos, making assessments that position the "colonial" and the "decolonial" in a binary that isolates European conquest as the watershed moment erases human history prior to the conquest of the Americas. I'm not rejecting the productive arguments, debates and scholarship about the historical epoch to which Mignolo (2002, 2007) refers as the advent of modernity/coloniality. For me, and for the work I tend to gravitate toward, the imaginary is real precisely because it creates the materialist conditions. Without the imaginary, the decolonial occludes so much and expunges, for example, brown imaginaries of desires and pleasures. As a brown, queer, gender-nonconforming butch, I continue to privilege critiques that embrace brown, feminist, queer/trans imaginaries to discern desires and pleasure.[120] When so much is discounted, as if it did not exist, and only the "real" that can be experienced through quantifiable, visible, measurable and physical conditions is taken into account, then we are right back at hindering methodologies and theories of the decolonial. We are right back at exclusionary practices if we dismiss the imaginary as "only metaphoric" and hence not useful as a form of critique. For me, the decolonial can be shortsighted, antifeminist and anti-queer/trans when the imaginary of desires, pleasures, gestures, hope and rejuvenating language is suppressed and dismissed as inconsequential because only the "real" is real. And what is real if affect is obstructed from the arena of reality?

Say, for example, that I felt the racist, homophobic othering gazes when I walked into a room, but the majority white, cisgender folks denied that I felt racism and homophobia. For them, what I felt was not "real." Therein lies the hermeneutic power struggle. Whose interpretation is legitimated? Those in power, with power, inevitably rise up and dictate what is and what is not "real."[121]

If we are to persist in the argument about the decolonial impetus—e.g., "Let's decolonize our minds, our schools, our curriculum, our neighborhoods, our food, our genders, our religions, our land, our heteronormative/homonormative families and relationships, our health, our bodies, our hair," and so on—instead of addressing how we do that, if we can do it, why we must do it, I want to propose another facet and one that I believe resides within the imaginary with the potential to decolonize, dismiss, or eradicate oppressive regimes. For now, I'm calling the mechanism "the will to feel." Notice: I'm not saying the will to numb, or the will to be greedy, murderous, racist fucks, or the will to rape and sexually abuse. I'm inviting us to take a leap into willingness that feels our collective, public lives while acknowledging our subjectivity. Each person feels differently, just as we know differently and integrate knowledge differently.

Let me begin with a personal story, my own phenomenology of spirit and mind that compelled me to linger upon will and willingness.[122] In September 2017, I witnessed my daughter drop twenty-two pounds in the span of four weeks. In a way, she eluded her will to live, choosing instead to control calories, defy hunger and entertain suicide. She had lost her appetite. No hunger, no craving, no life. No will. She fluctuated between depression and anger, and the only will she had was her willfulness to defy the very thing that would keep her alive—food. Her heart rate dropped so drastically that she had to be monitored nightly in the hospital for over a week. Only eleven years old, she had become a statistic, part of an epidemic that overwhelms this First World nation of ours filled with hypocrisy and contradictions.

Eat but don't get fat. Consume food, drugs, alcohol, bright shiny things—but don't gain weight, don't be an addict, don't be greedy. Be sexy but don't be sexual. Abide by patriarchal double standards that still press down upon you in the twenty-first century despite the decades of the 1960s and 1970s that attempted to advance rights for women, girls, LGBT folks, people of color, those on the margins. We made some headway but have regressed since the election of number 45. Eating disorders continue to rise and have not been tackled or resolved since they first received national attention in the 1970s. The media have given minimal regard to the disorder and only place at its center young, white, middle-class girls. I discovered after seven weeks in Children's Hospital of Denver that although most patients in the unit were girls from nine to eighteen years old, many of them white and middle-class, there were also Latinas, girls from working-class backgrounds with single mothers, and a teen girl from Africa.[123] There were also a few teenage boys, including one from Mexico. The boys presented as somewhat queer but clearly had no permission to present in anything other than the white, cisgender heteronormative, far-right Christianity of intolerance seemingly practiced by their families. I have no intention of speaking at length on anorexia or about my daughter. I will say that therapy—both family and individual—gave us the tools to be willing to heal, and she has demonstrated a willingness to face the monsters in her head.

My point in raising this brief, personal narrative is to introduce the notion of will in its various forms as I make an argument for the will to feel within the brown imaginary: will, willfulness, willful subjects, willingness, will to power, will to know, will to truth, will to live.[124] Nietzsche (1901) famously articulated the "will to power," described by Levinas (1990) as "an ideal that simultaneously brings with it its own form of universalization: war and conquest."[125] Foucault (2013) compelled us to consider the will to know and the will to truth, or we could say, the will to know the truth. We were challenged to become truth-seekers of knowledges, trying to discern how assorted disciplinary knowledges came to be. The will to live can be attributed to Schopenhauer, a philosopher I've not read closely and have only thought of in reference to a brief scene in the film *Frida* (2002). There is a clever moment when the scriptwriter invokes Frida's will to live after an accident that challenged her into yet more difference in an ableist world.[126] I ruminated about my own daughter's loss of a will to live and her resilient willfulness to individuate in ways harmful to her as she willfully toyed with death.[127]

In *Cruising Utopia*, José Esteban Muñoz (2009, 39) cites social theorists Theodor Adorno and Ernst Bloch, who remind us, "What is really important here is the will that it is different." What if the will to feel is the will to be different, as "feelings" compel us to express differently in a world that anticipates "logic," the "rational mind" and unfeeling to explain our lives, even when there is no logic, no rationale, no real explanation that can fulfill expectations grounded in that which is not part of one's experience, or phenomenological way of being. The fact is, however, that there is no hard and fast methodology, practice or theory that can avoid misuse, misinterpretation and misrepresentation.

The will to feel, I'm proposing, is its own hermeneutics, its own method and theory. At least, that is what I am attempting in this brief meditation that borrows from phenomenology to make my point. The phenomenology of first-person experience has a long history with various intellectuals, writers and philosophers. Chicana theorist Gloria Anzaldúa's methodologies of *autohistoria* and *autohistoria teoría* are phenomenological turns, and if we look to phenomenology as a method that "emphasizes the importance of lived experience" we may refer to Sara Ahmed in *Queer Phenomenology* (2006, 2). Lived experiences integrate the mind, body and psyche to cultivate new ways of knowing and being. These epistemologies and ontologies are born deep inside the body, beyond skin surfaces, beyond the superficial outer layers that are visible and easy to touch, beyond theories of the flesh, beyond what is merely seen but not grasped entirely because something is always hidden. (Like the imaginary which remains unseen and mutable, or like the psyche which remains unproven). The knowing is only a fragment of what lies beneath; the being is only a particle of what has been and what will be. What does it all mean then? Is the will to feel its own truth? Is there a way in which the will to feel encapsulates so much more than the sensory? So often we succumb to the urge to deaden the body to avert the excruciating pain of psychic, physical, emotional and historical trauma, which feels as real as present-day emotional abuse. What happens when we use those feelings, the woundedness and painful hurt, to drive critique and analysis consciously, with an astute awareness? That is to say, what happens when we implement affective emotions that move us to act or react in the first place? Are we only writing subjectivities, not rational, not Lockian or Western European Cartesian, but instead an argument and thesis guided by emotional affective intelligence grounded in willingness to feel what has shaped the mind/body/psyche? In *The Birth of Biopolitics*, Foucault posits that we must "[start] from the decision that universals do not exist, asking what kind of history can we do," instead of "using history as a critical method" that questions universals (2008, 1-3). In a sense, I am arguing that we turn to the will to feel as an antidote that strips away false notions of universal objective science. The rational mind can lie to itself and rely on objectivity as if one were not influenced by regionalism, history, culture, genders, sexualities, race and class background.

Decolonizing Imaginaries

If it is true that our deepest desires, feelings, and arousals are tapped into for imperial production, it also becomes crucial to ask how we might organize, mobilize, and form alternative

intimacies and desires. These are the intimacies that form the core of decolonizing imaginaries, those that understand sexual freedom only through collective self-determination.
—Anna M. Agathangelou, M. Daniel Bassichis and Tamara L. Spira, "Intimate Investments"

What does it mean to decolonize desire, if desire lives inside imaginaries, for example? Are the interstitial, the in-between, Nepantla and the impasse all ways of shifting inside of the decolonial enough to want to achieve a new kind of desire? Am I succumbing to colonialist conditioning or decolonial desire when or if I desire difference that is not a brown femme body, my gender of choice? What is it to desire the other? What is it to desire difference that embodies power, privilege, racial supremacy or gendered dominance? Can we just call it false consciousness or unconscious desire and be done with it? What is the path to decolonial desire? Is it even possible, given our histories of conquest, colonization and white supremacy in the United States? Maybe we're asking the wrong question when we ask how we decolonize desire. Perhaps desire cannot be colonized or decolonized or staged as postcolonial, for that matter. What if desire's history lies within the realm of the imaginary invoked from memory? In other words, the history of our desire is imprinted with the body's memory, which will reenact that memory through the imaginary, restaging, reinscribing, perhaps freeing the body from inhibitions or trauma. In *The Biopolitics of Feeling*, Kyla Schuller (2018) posits that the biopolitical imagination is placed in binary oppositions that include "affecting and being affected" and "culture and biology." She argues that these false binaries, "whether social constructionist notions of race that privilege notions of malleable embodiment over fixed biologies or affect theories that fail to interrogate how representations of affective capacity function as a key vector of racialization, therefore remain within the biopolitical imaginary" (2018, 15). The racialized and gendered biopolitical imaginaries are always already established and hierarchized. It is as if we must consistently deconstruct that which is as it is to renegotiate how it came to be as we live outside and inside that conventional box or trope or category, as we barter what presses down upon our desires.

Desire takes many forms, after all. What happens when we become fixated on the hegemonic, white colonialist, necro-political heterosexuality that is so pervasive? Can desire ever be truly authentic? Desire, with its fluidity, goes where it goes. It is free-floating and attaches itself to another and when it does, when desire moves and flees to that someone or something else, there is no stopping desiring bodies. The desiring body overwhelms the mind, persuading the heart perhaps and ignoring the psyche, the spirit-soul that says, no, don't do it. Do not allow desire to dictate who or what you will pursue when that someone or something is outside the realm of a semblance of sanity. But desire is not sane or rational. The persistent desiring body nags, craves, longs, lusts and is unwilling to let go of a fantasy fueled within and by the imaginary.

And when we let go, the patterns are repeated. The unconscious desiring body craves instant gratification only to sink into boredom once the craving is satisfied. Until the next time. How does one stop the pattern imprinted on the flesh of the desiring body, especially because the mind knows better; the mind rationalizes itself into something else, into an elsewhere that will not be. But the desiring body wants what it wants and the mind follows. The psyche-spirit-imaginary is persuaded persistently by the mind-body, which desires jointly.[128] The psyche-spirit-imaginary, however, knows better and goes along to teach a lesson, goes along and quietly assesses and watches and waits. The lesson will come. Call it karma, call it a soul lesson, call it a teachable moment. It's all the same, more or less. The pain in the body will remember that desire will neither be fulfilled nor be satisfied. Instead, desire will long and crave and sink into excruciating pain lodged in the heart, in the gut and in every nerve ending while plummeting deep into an invisible psyche.[129] What happens when you tap into the depths of those feelings? Do you ask yourself, when will the pain move through me and out again? Despite the brief moment of satisfied longing, the shared intimacies, desire can go elsewhere. And when it does? The energy moves and transpires elsewhere, cathecting, as it were, onto something or someone else. And why? Boredom, perhaps. Or time to move on for whatever reason—whether one feels misused or misjudged or mistreated with the life one has woken up to in a suburban flat or house. *This is not my beautiful house,* you hum to yourself as you enter the driveway, eager to escape the life you have built. The beautiful, perfect life that you no longer want. Where did that desire go? It evaporated from that one place or person and like a wave of steam, drifted to another. And then you realize, there is no shared alchemy of deep intimacy, meaning there can be no "real" desire because desire's imaginary is entranced by something else that can never really be, never having been. With no truths, no intimacies, is sex anything other than exercise? (I'm not judging the need for exercise.) And yet still you/I miss surface effects, surfacing affects. And then nothing. Perhaps you crave the intimacy of language and words? When desire is only satisfied with surface affects, the touch and arousal of nerve endings, the body's sensations relish that touch—like eating an apple pie—hot, warm, freshly baked. The instant the pie touches the tongue, pleasure is satisfied. And then it's time to move on to the next sensation that will satisfy the desiring, hungering body. Always the next thing to devour. And desires float and drift; desire is on the prowl, searching, reinventing, longing for that next fresh thing to satisfy craving for that instant, and the instant passes and prowling resurfaces to satisfy another fleeting hunger. Repeat, recycle, recreate and drag yourself along into more of the same until sheer monotony overwhelms you because the flesh's pleasure will never be enough. The flesh is only one thing, one small element of who and what we are. And yet the thinking, feeling body will want again and again what it cannot have.

The Impasse as Desire's Imaginary

What of the impasse? That interstitial remedy that seemingly stops time? To be inside, in the middle, in between, when all else is neither here nor there but everywhere. Let's ruminate about the impasse briefly to see if it can offer up anything new or fresh to desire's imaginary. If we take Ann Cvetkovich's understanding of feelings as "intentionally imprecise, retaining the ambiguity between feelings as embodied sensations and feelings as psychic or cognitive experiences" (2012, 22), then we can begin to understand the ephemeral impasse that could explain for us some form of desire.

For the brown queer/trans imaginary, the "good life," à la Lauren Berlant, has always been the fantasy to mock. While day-to-day life is about relishing the "impasse" of episodic events like *quinceañeras, fiestas* and *bodas*, for the brown queer/trans imaginary, the cultural measures must be transposed, inverted and reinterpreted to have queer/trans meaning. The "good life" is the fantasy inverted. Berlant persuasively illustrates the mind games that sustain the good life, and within that "attrition of fantasy" (2011, 11) we experience "the impasse" as "a stretch of time in which one moves around with a sense that the world is at once intensely present and enigmatic" (4). I am intrigued with the manner in which writers, theorists, philosophers and spiritual mystics theorize about that in-between space, the impasse, the interstices, Nepantla, the (decolonial) imaginary, impermanence—all point to a similar "stretched out present" because it is a present that cannot be ignored or evaded.

And what of colonial wounds, colonial feelings and colonial genders?[130] Do they live inside the impasse, inside Nepantla? If so, can the imaginary free up those wounds, those feelings, those gen-

ders and address them in a way that can be freeing from a past that
may be reinscribed with pleasure? In her posthumously published
book *Light in the Dark/Luz en lo Oscuro*, Anzaldúa asserts that

> Wounds cause you to shift consciousness—they either
> open you to the greater reality normally blocked by your
> habitual point of view or else shut you down, pushing you
> out of your body. Like love, pain might trigger compas-
> sion—if you're tender with yourself, you can be tender to
> others. Why not use pain as a conduit to recognizing an-
> other's suffering, even that of the one who inflicted pain
> wounding is the entrance to the sacred. (2016, 153)

If indeed we are prepared to embrace pain in its multiple it-
erations, perhaps we can transform it into newness. And what
happens when we follow the threads of hurt, pain, rage and re-
sentment? Sometimes we need to sink into the depths of the
wounds before we can climb out of the hole we may have deliberately fallen into. How do we know when to climb out of a hole
filled with our rage and self-satisfied hurt?[131] Are we nurturing
these wounds, colonial wounds as it were, that prohibit another
kind of desire? Or do they prohibit? Perhaps the wounds are the
opening to sacred desire. Perhaps these residual colonial wounds
entice a brown desiring imaginary, willful and willing, pushing us
to new realms of psychic/sexual pleasures previously negated and
judged as shameful because they are not the "norm." As brown
desiring bodies, queer and trans bodies, we succumb to an imaginary vexed with hurt and pain, hoping to transform ourselves by
venturing into the unknown where sensuous "queer gestures" and
"sexual futures" reside (Rodríguez 2014).[132]

Conclusion

How history imprints the mind, body, psyche: we can't escape our past, the memories that assemble us. I spent fourteen

years in the state of Colorado, and still, every time I gazed out of my bedroom window and saw traces of the first snow caught on dry branches of shrubs, I didn't see snow. I saw cotton—white fluffy cotton ready to be picked. Snow was not part of my body's psyche. I spent well over a decade longing to leave cold Colorado winters, and instead of seeing snow, I saw cotton fields from home. Why raise this? I simply want to reaffirm the power of memory and how that memory constructs the feelings that shape our thinking bodies. A biopolitical imaginary commands a leading role in what and how we interpret our world within a stubborn impression. Instead, I'm calling for the will to feel the imaginary beyond the restrictions we've inherited. How we remember shapes who we will be, our will to be, our will to feel in ways we've inherited in this lifetime.

I have been arguing that the will to feel is its own truth. To use those feelings, the woundedness, the hurt within an impasse, within that in-between imaginary drives a compassionate critique with a potential to transform us. Can the will to feel move us to act, resist and build a new way of being in a world that is in crisis? Are we willing to endeavor an imaginary in which hate and fear do not dictate the massacre of brown and black people? Are we willing to engage historical trauma, feel its tragedies and pleasures, to build something new?

Trio

When you stepped off the train, I hadn't expected you. I was by coincidence walking through the station to the vendor who sold my evening newspaper and as I clutched the paper under my arm, I locked eyes with, not you, but another woman. Her friend, a bearded man, scanned the magazines while she glimpsed my face, her gaze lasting a moment longer than is considered appropriate for strangers. I smiled courteously, spun around, and there you were. Moonlight in your chestnut hair? No. How could there be? We were inside a murky train station; we were underground. We were running from all that was above and beyond the city and its urban sprawl. Or, should I say, I was escaping you. But here you were. In my station.

You stepped down from the rail car, offering your left hand, and I noted the gold band on the third finger. I licked your palm and said, "You're here." In eyeglasses small and oval you hid dark eyes. I recognized your confident uncertainty. You pulled away, grazed my shoulder and kissed my mouth—a furtive kiss.

"It's okay. No one cares down here," I said.

I picked up your suitcase, the one you brought each time you came to see me. You wanted to surprise me, and I suppose you did. I spent the year convincing myself we were through.

"What's this?" I pointed to your ring.

"Nice suit," you said and scrutinized my frame. "Your father's?"

You removed your sunglasses, disguised no more and kissed me again. Candidly. I wanted to believe your kiss. But instead, I simulated happiness, convinced I'd found my way, devoid of deceitful kisses. You suspected otherwise. That's why you'd come. To tempt me with your desert, the hot sun's blinding light. Already I preferred the shadows of the city, its towering buildings reflecting transient clouds on glass windows cracked by subtle winds.

Just a short year ago I'd returned from Spain, Granada in the south. The Alhambra's vibrant yellows and shrill blues burst through me. I'd returned after peering into pools on moonlit nights; my own reflection frightened me. My face, as young as when we'd met, had no wrinkles, no strands of gray hair shimmered in that water. At the train station, I leapt out of the car and searched but you weren't there. *"She didn't come, she didn't come, of course she didn't come,"* I mumbled and remembered how you taunted even when you weren't present. Before I'd left, you'd said plainly and without regret, *"I never dream about you anymore. I'm sorry if that hurts but I don't think of you that way." "In what way?"* I asked but my questions remained habitually unanswered.

"Here." I fumbled in my jacket pocket and handed you a trinket I'd carried for the year I hadn't see you.

You glanced at the gift, a silver jewelry box, and dumped it in your coat pocket. We walked past newsstands, climbed up stairs and into city lights that made you lose your balance. I stopped before you, pulled your sunglasses from your pocket and put them on your face.

"Better?" I asked.

You nodded.

A street waif approached us and you didn't run or draw back afraid. You paused and studied him, a boy in tattered clothes, and when you tapped his unkempt hair, a neon light above us flickered and a halo crowned his tiny head.

"Be careful, *m'ijo*," I said and handed him a fifty-dollar bill. He escaped down a dim alley, his nimble footsteps echoed, the halo glinted faintly.

In your hotel room, you undressed and flung your naked body on the bed covering your breasts with a thin sheet. Your side swept tresses swung from one cheek to the other. As you palmed the silver box and opened the lid, a tiny silver heart tumbled to your lap.

"Ah. *Un milagro*," you said and twisted the heart with slim, deft fingers then dropped the worthless charm back in the box. I stared at the closed lid and felt nothing.

"You know what I learned about you? *¿En España?*" I asked.

"*¿Qué?*" You smirked.

I crawled next to you and propped myself up on my elbow, stretching out above the covers, naked and exposed. A thin moonbeam peeked through a crack between the curtains. We had ordered room service. It was what we did when we met. Sequestered in a hotel room, we ordered our meals, drank coffee and wine, slept erratically and avoided outsiders. I was with someone who never noticed I escaped to other women. You were with someone who trailed you.

"*Nada. Absolutamente nada.*"

You peered out from under the cover, and through the translucent bedsheet, your lips curved into a smile so self-assured that I wanted to slap you. Instead, I yanked the gold bracelet on your wrist. You jerked your hand away and tossed your hair; the trinket jingled and rattled against the headboard.

"Ouch," you said.

"Come on," I said, "let's go. This room's getting stuffy."

"Not yet," you said and inched closer.

I backed away but you nudged against me until I was on the bed's edge and there you rolled on top, smothering me. I wanted you; I always have and suspect I always will allow you to choke me with hot breath, your sheath across my neck, down to my nipples and between my legs. And when you pinched my thighs and thrust your way into me, I came back to you, and that you saw annoyed me. You grinned, smugly. I reached down and bit your nipple. You fell back and smiled having won another round.

I rested my head on your leg.

Your fingers in my hair, you said, "why won't you ask?"

"Ask what?"

"Where I was."

"Where you were?"

"That day."

"What day?"

"The day you returned."

"From Spain?"

"From Spain."

"*No me importa.*"

"Not even curious?"

"*Para nada.*" I rose from bed.

On the back wall, a cockroach crept up the ceiling. I slid into my slacks, pulled on my jacket and slipped my hand into an empty pocket. The silver box sat on the nightstand. I watched you dress.

We stumbled weak-kneed down the stairs to the lobby, bumping shoulders. A clerk at the front desk shouted your name, causing guests to gawk and your cheeks to grow crimson. You bowed your head, and when he handed you a piece of paper, you crammed it in your purse. We wandered into drizzling rain and you raced ahead, rustling for the paper and as you read its contents, you grinned. I lagged behind, caught up and hooked your arm in mine. I steered you toward my café.

It was there we saw Ricardo. Ricardo in loose black pants and tight black t-shirt with hair slicked back and wet. In black boots with thick heels, he swerved and faced us. You frowned at his scuffed boots.

"Ricardo's an old friend," I said.

"I *know* all your friends," you said.

"*Cuidado*, Pilar. You sound jealous," I said.

He and I kissed each other's cheeks, and he leaned in, but you stretched out your hand. Ricardo took it and squeezed. You twitched conspicuously as if to say he wasn't your type but I knew better.

"Will you dance tonight, Ricardo?"

He stomped a one-two-three rhythm four times on each heel and his steps echoed on the wooden floor. "In the back room. Come."

"Ricardo's from Sevilla," I whispered.

We followed him through a dark hallway, passed the café owner at the coffee bar and as he lifted his head to greet me, he ogled your breasts. You smiled and he returned a leer and I became the jealous one.

The café attracted local artists, dancers and poets, performers of the moment. Paintings and photographs on the walls exhibited the bohemian flair you'd once needed. When you saw my photograph in the corridor, you paused. A black-and-white photo of boulders had in its foreground an ocotillo cactus, spiny and tall and blooming. It was your desolate landscape with gaps and blanks; miles and miles of monochrome shades transcended into sublime brown hues. Like a child you peeked from behind a boulder, having mastered each cactus, each creature. Lizards that dared to run in your path could not have suspected your proclivity to chase them, seize their tales and hang them upside down. Their limbs outstretched, dangled and boxed at air. I was behind the lens, recording your misdeeds. Tabulating.

I left that desert to find this café and Ricardo, *el sevillano*, who listened when I vowed I was done counting the times you'd lied, cheated or robbed what I'd already given you, took more than you needed or could ever use. Ricardo rubbed his pock-marked cheeks with his palms, smoothing up and down repeatedly; his lips puckered until he completed a thorough massage, and he would say, *"That was not love. She does not deserve your tor-*

ment, my friend. She played you. Like a toy. Her little doll. Forgive me, but someone had to tell you." He'd throw his hands up, palms out and rise from his chair to pour more wine or espresso into our cups. He wasn't handsome necessarily with receding hair and craters in his cheeks, and his stout body resembled a wrestler's, not a dancer's. We drank wine and espresso and then more wine late into the night, pondering about the home we thought we wanted and neither had. Ricardo would point a thick finger at me and say, *"Go to Southern Spain, Valeria. You will see colors like never before. You will feel alive again,"* and he'd wave his finger. *"She is a woman to reckon with. She will cheat you, lie to you and take until there is no more for the taking, but she will have given you something you can never forget. The ghost of a contemptible past will show itself and that phantom will seek absolution. You will see. And all the while, she will suckle you, my friend,"* and then he'd snicker. And so, I did. I went to Spain to fall in love with shades and hues that only reminded me of you.

"Sit. Please sit." Ricardo ordered.

You tensed your lips when he pulled out your chair and placed a demitasse of espresso on the table before me. Just then, two women, poised on a wooden platform, swiveled their hips and called out to Ricardo. He glided to the platform and stood between them, grabbing each by an arm. I was expecting flamenco but heard the notes of an accordion, sentimental and melancholic. Deliberate and unhurried, three agile bodies shuffled to the tempo. Ricardo and two women maneuvered without losing time, without losing step, interlacing bodies in and out, back and forth in a pattern that seemed so simple, so easy, each one corresponding without speaking. I was captivated but not you, Pilar. You gaped at a napkin. You ripped off miniature pieces from the edges of the square, concentrating as if nothing could disturb you. I observed from the corner of my eyes, but I focused on the tango. The twists, the turns, the grappling arms, the tangling legs, all controlled skill. I admired the finesse.

Mistaken that the music was about to end, you pressed your lips against my ear. "Can we leave? *Por favor.*"

"In a minute," I mouthed, and you continued shredding paper, inching closer to its center from the edges.

Your hair hid your eyes and your mouth curved down at the corners in a crescent moon. The accordion wrapped up in a one-two beat, and Ricardo and the women pressed together, huddling. After the women disappeared through the door from which they had entered, Ricardo slid to our table.

"You devil. You didn't tell me you were dancing tango."

"I know, I know, but I was unsure of the steps. And handling two women at once is no easy task, my friend." He winked and I laughed.

"I'm better at this." Ricardo stomped his boots confidently to flamenco accents.

"You dance like a champion," I said.

Ricardo grinned, looked at you and back at me, and we raised our eyebrows in unison.

"And your partners?" I attempted to distract myself from your impertinence.

"Ah. Laura *y* Liliana. Beautiful dancers. You want to meet them?"

You glared at me and said to him, "We're leaving."

"Another time, Ricardo," I winked.

Outside the rain subsided. We strolled in silence, and when we arrived at your hotel, the clerk called out and handed you another message.

You read and said aloud, "I have to go."

"Now?"

"Yes. Now. Tonight."

We climbed the stairs to your room, and you fumbled with the room key, which I took and jiggled in the lock until the door crashed opened. Inside, you kicked off your shoes and each banged against the wall. Unzipping your skirt, it dropped to the floor and you slinked in a silk, white slip; your belly's flesh bulged slightly, round and lush. You lit a cigarette and paced the floor, in nylon feet. I sprawled out on the bed, shoes on, fully clothed. I waited for your mood to change.

"Come back with me," you said and stopped pacing.

I ignored you.

"*Ándale*," you said almost sweetly.

I shook my head with a patience I didn't know I had.

"*Por favor. Valeria. Por favor.*"

Again, I shook my head.

You ran and slammed the bathroom door. I heard the bath water running and buried my face in your pillow, breathing the evening's stale perfume.

"*Ay*, Pilar," I muttered and fell asleep.

An hour had passed when I awoke to stirring in the dark. You dressed by moonlight, and your eyes were moist, your cheeks glistened. I stood, picked up your packed bag and opened the door.

Outside a fine rain fell and you blinked mist from your eyelashes. In the station at the track outside your car, I held the silver jewelry box.

"Don't forget this," I said.

"Keep it."

"You sure?"

You nodded, boarded the train, and you were gone.

I wandered to the newsstand and saw the woman from before hovering with her bearded man, and as he scanned front-page headlines, she gazed at me and smiled. Discreetly. I returned the smile overtly. He seized her elbow, guiding her up the stairs, and she twisted around and nodded toward the vendor, who held a slip of paper that he waved to me as if to say, *She left this for you.*

I thanked him, took the note, crammed it in your silver box, placed the items on a ledge beside the track and walked away.

Notes

[1] In an essay that I wrote in 1982 on the Mexican anarchist group Partido Liberal Mexicano, I argued that the nation-nationalist class-based movement placed women-workers' exploitation in the forefront, but dismissed their oppression in the home and in their social-sexual relationships with the male leaders of the organization. The essay should have been published years ago, but "political" circumstances delayed it. In light of current debates spawned by deconstructionists, this essay is dated but perhaps useful because it analyzes the gender ideology within nationalist class-based movements. See Emma Peréz, "*A La Mujer*: A Critique of the Mexican Liberal Party's Ideology on Women," in *Between Borders: Essays on Mexicana/Chicana History*, ed. Adelaida Del Castillo (Los Angeles: Floricanto Press, 1990), 459-82. Also refer to my dissertation, *Through Her Love And Sweetness: Women, Revolution and Reform in Yucatan, 1910-1918*, Ph.D. dissertation, University of California, Los Angeles, 1988. Again, I point out that in a region where socialism was attempted, women's issues were only brought to the forefront to benefit a male political arena.

[2] For a historical materialist analysis of Chicano/Mexicano social movements see Mario Barrera, *Race and Class in the Southwest* (Notre Dame: Notre Dame Press, 1978), any number of essays by Juan GómezQuiñones, Tomás Almaguer and most recently, David Montejano, *Anglos and Mexicans in the Making of Texas, 1836-1986* (Austin: University of Texas Press, 1987). For studies by Chicanas who examine the primary place of gender along with a race and class analysis see, Patricia Zavella, *Women's Work and Chicano Families* (Ithaca: Cornell University, 1987) and Vicki Ruiz, *Cannery Women, Cannery Lives* (Albuquerque: University of New Mexico, 1987). Also refer to Deena González, *The Women of Santa Fe*, Ph.D. dissertation,

University of California, Berkeley, 1986 and essays by Antonia Castañeda, Beatrice Pesquera and Denise Segura.

[3] Heidi Hartmann's essay elucidates the antiquated, unresolved debate. See H. Hartmann, "The Unhappy Marriage of Marxism and Feminism: Towards a More Progressive Union," in *Women and Revolution,* ed. Lydia Sargent (Boston: South End Press, 1981), 2-41. I refuse to identify myself as a "Marxist" and prefer "socialist" because Marxist identifies one with a male, Mr. Karl Marx. While I sanction Mr. Marx's theories and writings, I prefer to call my method a socialist feminist or historical materialist one.

[4] Chicano Studies departments that have existed for ten years or more and still have not hired and tenured Chicanas are embarrassments to our community. Lip service.

[5] Julia Kristeva discussed her hope for Chinese women and China's potential for a different revolution that acknowledged women. She found a strong, female affirming atmosphere in China. See Kristeva, *About Chinese Women,* trans. Anita Barrows (London: Boyars, 1977). That was before the massacre in Tiananmen Square in 1989. Kristeva, however, reevaluated her Marxism before this massacre. Within weeks of the Tiananmen Square debacle, the women in Nicaragua suffered a blow to their movement when President Daniel Ortega urged them to place women's issues aside for the revolution, as if women's struggle and the revolution are mutually exclusive. The same time-worn debates.

[6] I owe my development of socialist feminist theory to works by Juliet Mitchell, particularly *Women's Estate* (New York: Vintage, 1973), still a superb little book and to Michele Barrett, *Women's Oppression Today* (London: Verso, 1988), where she discusses the significance of gender ideology. Numerous socialist feminist writings generated my analysis, but in my Chicana community historians Deena González, Antonia Castañeda and the Chicana scholars of MALCS help me to imagine our specific, organic movement, especially through our organization. MALCS, Mujeres Activas en Letras y Cambia Social, was founded in 1982 in Northern California by a handful of Chicana academicians eager to affirm our Chicana network within the University.

[7] As a historical materialist, I am aware that theory follows practice, but as a socialist feminist I probe theory to apply what is useful and disregard the rest.

[8] I agree with Leslie Wahl Rabine, who argues that "Lacanian psycho-analysis is, I think, of greater interest and use to feminist theory than Derridean deconstruction and, not surprisingly, feminists have a much more intense relation of ambivalence and outrage to this theory." See "A Feminist Politics of Non-Identity," *Feminist Studies,* 14:1 (Spring 1988): 11-31. Refer to footnote 25. For me French feminists' deconstruction of Lacanian psychoanalysis is useful for feminist theory on sexuality. I also want to point out the importance of Gayatri Chakravorty Spivak's deconstructive essays on colonialism and feminism. For the purpose of this essay, I rely on theoreticians who discuss sexuality directly. For me that is Luce Irigaray. I believe Irigaray's examination of sexuality may provide lesbians with a language to decode our oppression, then invert the language with our command.

[9] In the late 1970s, I was revitalized by the women in the organization, Lesbians of Color, active in Los Angeles from about 1978 to 1982. We were a network of Latinas and Black lesbians who marched in political rallies and supported each other through daily endeavors. See Cherrie Moraga and Gloria Anzaldúa, cds., *This Bridge Called My Back: Writings by Radical Women of Color* (Watertown, Mass.: Persephone Press, 1981; 2d ed. New York: Kitchen Table Press, 1983).

[10] I use this term, *un sitio y una lengua,* to emphasize that as Chicanas we have always had this space and language, however we assert it now in our exclusive organizations for women of color. For Chicana academicians, the organization is, of course, MALCS, where we create for each other.

[11] I realize this is ambiguous, but what I mean to say is that I believe that we can each remember a childhood memory that either drew us to, or pulled us away from, people who could be a "love object." This is not a judgment or criticism about people's choices, but rather an explanation, a Chicana lesbian historical materialist explanation. I have discussed these core issues at length with Deena González and Antonia Castañeda and we hope to publish our conjectures soon.

[12] To quote Latina feminist, Lourdes Arguelles, "the person today who is homophobic is a criminal." From her panel discussion on "Latinas and AIDS" at the National Association for Chicano Studies, Los Angeles, March 31-April 2, 1989.

[13] I use the definition of discourse put forth by the editors Elaine Marks and Isabelle De Courtivron, *New French Feminisms* (Amherst: University of Massachusetts Press, 1980), 3. Discourse is "the relation between language and the object to which it apparently refers," e.g. how women have been written about.

[14] Luce Irigaray, *Speculum of the Other Woman,* trans. Gillian G. Gill, (Ithaca: Cornell University Press, 1985), 81. Further reference to this work will be found in the text.

[15] "Gaze," in Freud's terms, "As phallic activity linked to the anal desire for sadistic mastery of the object." The "love of looking" and the sadistic male are hence linked to violence in pornography. Toril Moi, *Sexual/Textual Politics* (New York: Routledge, 1985), 134. Also see Irigaray, *Speculum,* 47.

[16] Jacques Lacan, *Ecrits,* trans. Alan Sheridan (London: Tavistock, 1977).

[17] Helene Cixous; "Castration or Decapitation?" *Signs* 7:1 (Autumn 1981): 46.

[18] I want to stress that the French feminists are *not* arguing that "biology is destiny" anymore than Freud or Lacan argue this. The value of their work is that they understand that female and male are socially constructed. British Marxist-feminist Juliet Mitchell best argued this in her study, *Psychoanalysis and Feminism* (Harmondsworth: Penguin, 1974), and she was chided for her position in the 1970s. I think we are closer to accepting the value of psychoanalysis in that it provides an understanding of the male-symbolic-order-patriarchy. I argue that an examination of the Oedipal triangle and the primal scene can release us finally from its enslavement, from women's and men's addiction/dependency to the patriarchy.

[19] Xaviere Gauthier, "Is there Such a Thing as Women's Writing?" in *NewFrenchFeminisms,* 162. Gauthier argues that women accept the phallic system to "find their place in male language, law, grammar, syntax." They become "completely divorced from themselves without knowing it." They go crazy denying themselves to accommodate male definitions of what women should be—more like men but still unlike them. The double-messages and double-binds make us appear irrational and hysterical.

[20] Jeffrey Weeks, *Sex, Politics and Society: The Regulation of Sexuality since 1800* (London: Longman Group Limited, 1981), 7.

21 Michel Foucault, *The History of Sexuality: Volume I, An Introduction* (New York: Pantheon Books, 1978).

22 Ibid. p. 48. I read the English translation; therefore, the translator may be the culprit. The original may or may not be far from its English translation, but it is disconcerting that the translation should read as such.

23 I am reminded of a male friend who asked if I enjoyed the film, *Dangerous Liaisons*. I responded that I thought it was misogynist, to which he queried, "But, didn't you enjoy it?" He may well have said "Forget the fact that it was a rape, didn't you enjoy it anyway." I refuse to indulge myself in Hollywood's interpretation of male-female sexual power relations. Even when Hollywood attempts to make a "feminist" film like *The Accused,* about a woman's brutal gang-rape, the filmmakers rely on the fact that the male audience will practice their "gaze," not at all interested in the weak feminist message.

24 Perhaps he clarifies this omission in the other volumes, but I doubt that he appropriates a feminist analysis.

25 The fusion of sex and power is the foundation for violence against all women and children and men of color. Lynchings, whippings, beatings and murder of black and brown-skinned men must also be addressed when discussing sexual power relations. I will not do so at any length but I recognize the sociohistorical brutality against men of color and how this damages their psyche and the psyche of our community. When men of color become perpetrators against women and children, and many do, I lose compassion and patience, however.

26 Linda Gordon has written an excellent study about child abuse in the nineteenth-century United States, a different aberration from late twentieth-century sexual molestation cases.

27 Historian Deena González argues, "If we conceptualize most history as written by white males from a white male perspective, then we must start with the premise that it is all biased history." I agree with González's premise that Chicana historians are forced to deconstruct what has been written before we can reconstruct our own history. Small wonder that our work takes longer to produce. See Gregg Mitchell, "Barrier Crusaders," *Pomona College Today* (Summer 1989): 17, for González's quote.

[28] For those of you who are already incensed with my use of the Oedipal complex to explain Spanish conquest, I ask that you remain patient and remember that this is about a process which looks at psychoanalysis to move on and away from it ultimately.

[29] Octavio Paz, *The Labyrinth of Solitude*, trans. Lysander Kemp (New York: Grove Press 1961), 65-88. I refer of course to his chapter on "La Chingada," where he denigrates the Aztec princess, Malintzin Tenepal. Adelaida Del Castillo's criticism of Paz's ahistorical account of Malintzin still stands up well. See her essay in *Essays on La Mujer*, ed. Rosaura Sánchez (Los Angeles: Chicano Studies Research Center, 1977). I will not reiterate this history; I assume most already know it. Many Chicana scholars have responded to Paz's misogyny at some point. To list all of the essays, publications and private gripes is a pointless exercise. Take my word for it. Or, ask any Chicana about Paz's *chingada*. I do recommend Norma Alarcón's essay, "Chicana Feminist Literature: A Re-vision through Malintzin/or Malintzin: Putting Flesh Back on the Object" in *This Bridge Called My Back*, 182-190. Alarcón argues, and I agree, that we must also delve into the psychosexual exploitation of women of color along with exposing economic exploitation. See also Alarcón's "Traddutora, Traditora: A Paradigmatic Figure of Chicana Feminism," in *Cultural Critique*, 13 (Fall 1989): 57-88.

[30] On Lacan see *Sex, Politics and Society*, 3-4.

[31] Tzetvan Todorov explains the significance of symbols as miscommunication between Spaniards and the Aztecs. Spaniards assumed they understood Aztec symbols and actions and, of course, they did not. Refer to Todorov, *The Conquest of America*, trans. Richard Howard (New York: Harper and Row Publishers, 1982).

[32] Skin color, however, plays an important factor. The lighter the skin, the more possible it is to pass through doors of power and privilege. Of course, skin color gradations when one has the white skin and the white name of a white father and a mestiza for a mother, then one is likely to have access to more power in a racist society. What one does with that power politically is a different issue altogether and not one I wish to debate. Of course, class status is also a prominent factor to consider in these matchings.

[33] For Chicanos, their maleness offers them the male language since childhood. They must learn to master the colonizer male dialogue, however.

[34] Chicana scholars in literature and theater have criticized Valdez's negative, one-dimensional depiction of women in his productions. I am interested in examining his choice as a symbol which perpetuates the law of the father. See, for example, Yolanda Broyles-González, "What Price 'Mainstream'? Luis Valdez's *Corridos* on Stage and Film," *Cultural Studies,* 4:3 (October 1990): 281-93.

[35] Irigaray, *Speculum,* 72. She discusses "the girl's turning to the father" to embrace "normal" femininity and "renounce phallic activity." For a young Chicana's account of rape and incest, see Arcelia Ponce, "*La preferida,*" *Third Woman* 4 (1989): 85-89.

[36] Antoinette Fouque, *New French Feminisms,* 117.

[37] Antonieta Castañeda's dissertation, Chapter 5.

[38] Numerous studies on sexual molestation and child abuse discuss this persistent pattern of addiction and dependency. I recommend the work by counseling psychologist, Charlotte Davis Kasl, *Women, Sex and Addiction: A Search for Love and Power* (New York: Ticknor and Fields, 1989). I particularly like Kasl's approach because she focuses upon moving beyond sexual damage to recovery and healing. For a new study on child abuse and its violent damage see Leonard Shengold, *Soul Murder: The Effects of Childhood Abuse and Deprivation* (New Haven: Yale University Press, 1989).

[39] Gloria Anzaldúa, a *tejana,* writes eloquently and vividly about her experience in Texan-Anglo schools. Refer to G. Anzaldúa, *Borderlands/La Frontera: The New Mestiza* (San Francisco: Spinsters/Aunt Lute, 1987). See chapter five, "How to Tame a Wild Tongue." I recommend the whole book, however.

[40] Marguerite Duras, *The Lover.* Trans. Barbara Bray. (New York: Harper & Row, 1985).

[41] Irigaray, *Speculum,* 27.

[42] Most of you know that the word in the song is "corazones," hearts, and that it was a fun joke to sing "calzones," underwear. Hah, what do you think of that, Dr. Freud?

[43] Emma Pérez, *Forgetting the Alamo, Or, Blood Memory.* University of Texas Press, 2009.

[44] Michel Foucault, *The History of Sexuality, Vol. I: An Introduction* (New York: Pantheon, 1978).

[45] Emma Pérez, *The Decolonial Imaginary: Writing Chicanas into History* (Bloomington: Indiana University Press, 1999), 5-7.

[46] Deena González, *Refusing the Favor: The Spanish Mexican Women of Santa Fe, 1820-1880* (New York: Oxford University Press, 1999); and José Esteban Muñoz, *Disidentifications: Queers of Color and the Performance of Politics* (Minneapolis: University of Minnesota Press, 1999).

[47] Martin Duberman, Martha Vicinus and George Chauncey Jr., eds., *Hidden from History: Reclaiming the Gay and Lesbian Past* (New York: New American Library, 1989); George Chauncey Jr., *Gay New York: Gender, Urban Culture, and the Making of the Gay Male World: 1890-1940* (New York: Basic Books, 1994); Elizabeth Lapovsky Kennedy and Madeline D. Davis, *Boots of Leather, Slippers of Gold: The History of a Lesbian Community* (New York: Routledge University Press, 1993); Lillian Faderman, *Odd Girls and Twilight Lovers: A History of Lesbian Life in Twentieth Century America* (New York: Columbia University Press, 1991); Randolph Trumbach, *Sex and the Gender Revolution: Heterosexuality and the Third Gender in Enlightenment London,* (Chicago: Chicago University Press, 1998); Lisa Duggan, *Sapphic Slashers: Sex, Violence, and American Modernity* (Durham: Duke University Press, 2000); and John Howard, *Men Like That: A Southern Queer History* (Chicago: Chicago University Press, 1999). Also worth noting is the San Francisco Lesbian and Gay History Project compiled by Liz Stevens and Estelle B. Freedman, which was produced as a video, *She Even Chewed Tobacco* (New York History Project, 1983). Susan Lee Johnson refers to one of the more prominent lesbians featured in the pictorial collection, a mixed-race Mexican-Anglo woman, Elvira Virginia Mugarrieta, also known as "Babe Bean," and Jack Garland, born in Stockton, California, in 1870. See Susan Lee Johnson, "'A Memory Sweet to Soldiers': The Significance of Gender," in *A New Significance: Re-envisioning the History of the American West,* ed. Clyde A. Milner II (New York: Oxford University Press, 1996), 255-78.

[48] González, *Refusing the Favor;* Ramon Gutiérrez, *When Jesus Came, the Corn Mothers Went Away: Marriage, Sexuality, and Power in New Mexico, 1500-1846* (Stanford: Stanford University Press, 1991); and Antonia Castañeda, "Sexual Violence in the Politics and Policies

of Conquest: Amerindian Women and the Spanish Conquest of Alta California," in *Building with Our Hands: New Directions in Chicana Studies,* ed. Adela de la Torre and Beatriz M. Pesquera (Berkeley: University of California Press, 1993), 15-33.

49 Siobhan B. Somerville, *Queering the Color Line: Race and the Invention of Homosexuality in American Culture* (Durham: Duke University Press, 2000), 3.

50 For fundamental background to the history of the Southwest, the making of the US-Mexico border and subsequent immigration laws, refer to Rodolfo Acuña, *Occupied America: A History of Chicanos,* 3rd ed. (New York: Harper and Row, 1988); Juan Gómez-Quiñones, *Roots of Chicano Politics, 1600-1940* (Albuquerque: University of New Mexico Press, 1994); David Gutierrez, *Walls and Mirrors: Mexican Americans, Mexican Immigrants, and the Politics of Ethnicity* (Berkeley: University of California Press, 1995); and Vicki L. Ruiz, *From Out of the Shadows: Mexican Women in Twentieth Century America* (New York: Oxford University Press, 1998).

51 El Paso County Court Records, 1881-1920, *The State of Texas v. Guadalupe Vega and Margarita R. Perez,* adultery, April 17, 1841, 887, University of Texas, El Paso Special Collections.

52 Deena González, "The Widowed Women of Santa Fe: Assessments on the Lives of an Unmarried Population, 1850-1880," in *On Their Own: Widows and Widowhood in the American Southwest, 1848-1939,* ed. Arlene Scadron (Champaign: University of Illinois Press, 1989).

53 Yolanda Retter, "On the Side of Angels: Lesbian Activism in Los Angeles, 1970-90" (Ph.D. diss., University of New Mexico, 1999); Yolanda Chavez Leyva, "Listening to the Silences in Latina/Chicana Lesbian History," in *Living Chicana Theory,* ed. Carla Trujillo (Berkeley: Third Woman Press, 1998); Deborah Vargas, "Cruzando Fronteras: Selena, Tejano Public Culture and the Politics of Cross-Over" (paper presented at the annual meeting of the American Studies Association, Washington, D.C., October 1997); and Maylei Blackwell, "Contested Histories and Retrofitted Memory: Chicana Feminist Subjectivities between and beyond Nationalist Imaginaries-An Oral History of the Hijas de Cuauhtémoc" (paper presented as qualifying essay, History of Consciousness: University of California, Santa Cruz, May 1997).

[54] Luz Calvo, "Postcolonial Queer Fantasies" (Ph.D. diss., University of California, Santa Cruz, 2000); Catriona Esquibel, *With Her Machete in Her Hand* (Austin: University of Texas Press, forthcoming); Sandra Soto, "Sexing Aztlan: Subjectivity, Desire and the Challenge of Racialized Sexuality in Chicana/o Literature" (Ph.D. diss., University of Texas, Austin, 2001); and Yvonne Yarbro-Bejarano, *The Wounded Heart: Writing on Cherríe Moraga* (Austin: University of Texas Press, 2001).

[55] Gloria Anzaldúa, *Borderlands/La Frontera: The New Mestiza* (San Francisco: Spinsters/Aunt Lute, 1987); and Herbert Eugene Bolton, *The Spanish Borderlands: A Chronicle of Old Florida and the Southwest* (New Haven: Yale University Press, 1921).

[56] Alicia Gaspar de Alba, *Sor Juana's Second Dream: A Novel* (Albuquerque: University of New Mexico Press, 1999); Alicia Gaspar de Alba, *The Mystery of Survival and Other Stories* (Arizona: Bilingual Press, 1993); John Rechy, *City of Night* (New York: Grove Press, 1963); and Arturo Islas, *The Rain God* (New York: Avon Books, 1991).

[57] Calvo, "Art Comes for the Archbishop: The Semiotics of Contemporary Chicana Feminism and the Work of Alma López," *Meridians: Feminism, Race, Transnationalism* 5, no. 1, (2004): 221. I'd like to point out that the title of the essay originated from Luz Calvo.

[58] Calvo, "Art Comes for the Archbishop," 201-224.

[59] Emma Pérez, *The Decolonial Imaginary: Writing Chicanas into History* (Bloomington: Indiana University Press, 1999), 121-122.

[60] See, for example, Jeannette Rodríguez, *Our Lady of Guadalupe: Faith and Empowerment among Mexican-American Women* (Austin: University of Texas Press, 1994); D. A. Brading, *Mexican Phoenix: Our Lady of Guadalupe: Image and Tradition across Five Centuries* (London: Cambridge University Press, 2003).

[61] Michel Foucault, *The History of Sexuality: An Introduction*, Volume 1 (New York: Vintage Books, 1980, 11, 34.

[62] "Depiction of the Virgin of Guadalupe Stirs Objections," Hollis Walker, Special to The Times, *Los Angeles Times,* 2001.

[63] "Santa Fe Madonna Sparks Firestorm," Sarah S. King, *Art in America,* June 2001

[64] "How Protests Make Blasphemy Unwelcome," John Horvat, II, (2007). http://www.tfp.org/TFPForum/Tendential_Revolution/santa_fe_chill.htm.

[65] Ada María Isasi-Díaz, *La Lucha Continues: Mujerista Theology* (Maryknoll, N.Y.: Orbis Books, 2004), 54.

[66] Ibid.

[67] "This is a sin and it is morally wrong, I think that you are a disgraceful bitch who has no respect for the one who crushes the serpent." Email: Edna Best October 4, 2001, Alma Lopez website: http://www.almalopez.net/ORemail/emails.html.

[68] Mary Rivera Griswold, *The New Mexican,* March 2001, Lopez website: http://www.almalopez.com. The artist, Alma Lopez, removed this quote and others like it from her website after continuing to receive threats from harsh critics.

[69] Email: Esperanza, November 25, 2002, Lopez website: http://www.almalopez.net/ORemail/emails.html.

[70] Teresa de Lauretis , *The Practice of Love: Lesbian Sexuality and Perverse Desire* (Bloomington: Indiana University Press,1994), 155.

[71] Michel Foucault, *The History of Sexuality: An Introduction*, 1978, 34.

[72] Email: José Villegas, March 18, 2001, Lopez website: http://www.almalopez.net/ORemail/emails.html.

[73] Email: Pedro Romero Sedeño to M.V. Sedano, February 9, 2002, López website: http://www.almalopez.net/ORemail/emails.html. See the ongoing, numerous messages that show the contrasting views between Sedeño and López in February 2002.

[74] Email: Pedro Romero Sedeño, Feb. 12, 2002, Lopez website: http://www.almalopez.net/ORemail/emails.html.

[75] Email: Pedro Romero Sedeño, February 2, 2002, Lopez website: http:// www.almalopez.net/ORemail/emails.html.

[76] Email: Pedro Romero Sedeño, May 10, 2002, Lopez website: http://www.almalopez.net/ORemail/emails.html.

[77] As an example of scholarship that challenges the European model, refer to Walter Mignolo, *Global Histories, Local Designs* (Princeton: Princeton University Press, 2000). For an intriguing fresh look at the violence emerging from European colonization, see Nelson Maldonado-Torres, *Against War*: (Durham, N.C.: Duke University Press, 2008). For an excellent feminist revision of Catholicism as a patriarchal institution, see Ada María Isasi-Díaz, *La Lucha Continues: Mujerista Theology* (Maryknoll, N.Y.: Orbis Books, 2004).

78 Email: Carlos Martinez, March 25, 2001, Lopez website: http://www.almalopez.net/ORemail/emails.html.

79 Email: Mike Gratz, May 22, 2001, Lopez website: http://www.almalopez.com/ORemail/em052201.html.

80 Email: Kevin Sorbanelli, September 29, 2005, Lopez website.

81 See *La Voz de Aztlán,* November 13, 2008, http://www.aztlan.net/homosexuals_sodomize_jesus_christ.htm.

82 Ibid.

83 Calvo, 204.

84 Consuelo Flores, March 26, 2001.

85 Yolanda Rael, December 11, 2001.

86 Email: Elvira Segura, October 30, 2002.

87 Email: Hector Alvarez, October 6, 2001.

88 Helen López, April 27, 2001.

89 Michel Foucault, *The Use of Pleasure: Volume 2 of the History of Sexuality, trans. Robert Hurley* (New York: Vintage Books, 1985), 4. The full quote: "In short, it was a matter of seeing how an 'experience' came to be constituted in modern Western societies, an experience that caused individuals to recognize themselves as subjects of a 'sexuality,' which was accessible to very diverse fields of knowledge and linked to a system of rules and constraints. What I planned, therefore, was a history of the experience of sexuality, where experience is understood as the correlation between fields of knowledge, types of normativity and forms of subjectivity in a particular culture." I find this passage particularly vital because Foucault claims to have abandoned the task of writing a history of sexuality that spoke to the experience of sexualities and how they were constructed by laws, religion, medical tracts, etc. Instead, he offered an analysis of ideologies and discourses that shaped sexualities and yet by doing so, he also put forth a valuable paradigm for writing the history of racialized sexualities.

90 I am employing "queer" as a term that includes lesbians, gays, transgender and bisexuals while acknowledging that many of those interviewed did not refer to themselves as queer but instead chose to be specific about their identities, whether racial, national or about their sexuality. None of these terms of self-identity are static and each transforms throughout history. Queer can also apply to heterosexuals who practice non-heteronormative sexualities. Transgender is more

current and perhaps the least understood. For an insightful look at transgender, see Judith Halberstam, *In a Queer Time and Place: Transgender Bodies, Subcultural Lives* (New York City: New York University Press, 2005). On page 53, he points out: "Transgender is for the most part a vernacular term developed within gender communities to account for the cross-identification experiences of people who may not accept all of the protocols and strictures of transsexuality. Such people understand cross-identification as a crucial part of their gendered self, but they may pick and choose among the options of body modification, social presentation and legal recognition available to them."

[91] Gregory Ramos interviewed twenty-five queers in El Paso, however there are twenty-four transcripts and/or tapes of the interviews. All are housed at the Institute of Oral History, University of Texas, El Paso and were conducted between 2000 and 2002. (The human subjects permission now necessary even for cultural studies are also on file at UTEP). He initially titled his performance piece "Border Voices" but has since revised the piece and calls it "Border Stories." A powerful one-man performance, Ramos melds the voices of the interviewees to show a complex life for queers on the border; some are HIV positive.

[92] Let me say a word about racial and national self-identity. Chicana/o came into being as part of a political project that emerged from the Chicana/o movements of the 1960s and 70s. Chicanas/os are of Mexican descent and live in the United States. While those who call themselves Chicana/o do not embrace "Hispanic," it is important to note that Hispanic, while riddled with problems, is a term of self-identity used by Mexican Americans and other Latinos who live in the United States. Latina/o has become an umbrella term of self-identity for all people of Latin American, Central American and Mexican descent who live in the United States. I have opted to use Chicana/o or Mexican since all but one of the interviewees are Chicana/o or Mexican. I make note of the one interviewee who identifies as "Hispanic."

[93] I am not assessing the oral interviews through a social science lens, although that kind of assessment is undeniably significant. I am interested in writing the narrative that speaks to the colonial bind for Chicana/o queers on the US-Mexico border, particularly in El Paso, Texas, who find themselves decolonizing through mere participation in their daily queer lives.

[94] There are hundreds of historical texts addressing Manifest Destiny and the battles of the Alamo and San Jacinto (1836) in which Coahuila y Tejas became the Texas Republic, followed by the US-Mexico War in 1846 when Texas and the southwestern states of New Mexico, Arizona and California specifically became occupied by the United States. For examples, see Rodolfo Acuña, *Occupied American: A History of Chicanos.* 3rd Edition, (New York: Harper and Row, 1988); Juan Gómez-Quiñones, *The Roots of Chicano Politics* (Albuquerque: University of New Mexico Press, 1994).

[95] Eithne Luibhéid, *Entry Denied: Controlling Sexuality at the Border* (Minneapolis: University of Minnesota, 2002), 4.

[96] The anti-immigration law, SB1070 in Arizona, permits yet another round of vicious hatred against Mexicans as we move into the twenty-first century.

[97] See Siobhan B. Somerville, *Queering the Color Line: Race and the Intervention of Homosexuality in American Culture (Durham: Duke University Press, 2000)* for an excellent argument regarding the 1986 Supreme Court case, *Plessy v. Ferguson,* which established a "separate but equal" clause legalizing the segregation of blacks from whites. At that same moment, the United States also established distinctions between heterosexual and homosexual. For an incisive discussion of eugenics on the US-Mexico Border, see Alexandra Stern, "Buildings, Boundaries, and Blood: Medicalization and Nation-Building on the US-Mexico Border, 1910-1930," *Hispanic American Historical Review* 79:1 (Feb. 1999): 41-81.

[98] Senator John C. Calhoun of South Carolina, in his speech before Congress in January 1847, argued against annexing all of Mexico because Mexicans were mestizos and Indians, both of whom were inferior to the pure, white race of Americans. See David Weber, *Foreigners in Their Native Land* (Albuquerque: University of New Mexico, 1977). In 1924, Samuel Holmes, a professor of Zoology at the University of Berkeley was a nativist who did not want more Mexicans entering the United States. He said: "You cannot let a foreign group into a country without its having the effect of keeping a great many thousand, perhaps millions, of our own native population from being born. Are you going to sacrifice our children for the sake of assimilating the Mexican?" In Mark Reisler, *By the Sweat of their Brow* (Berkeley: University of California Press, 1979).

[99] Recently that same thing has been identified as nothing more than liberal, civil rights under a capitalist socio-economy that allows queers to consume and live daily lives comfortably without much thought to "racial, gendered and sexual hierarchies of the nation-state" that must be understood as endemic to "the problems of the political economy." See David Eng with Judith Halberstam and José Munoz, "What's Queer About Queer Studies Now? *Social Text* 84-84, nos. 3-4 (2005), 1.

[100] What I mean by my use of imaginary is that it is much like the unconscious—that which exists but is difficult to trace since it has been accepted for so long as "normal."

[101] As I became more of a Foucauldian, I began to see how I could use his methods to unravel colonialist ideology. I came up with my notion of decolonizing history and a theoretical construct that I name the decolonial imaginary. To decolonize our history and our historical imaginations, we must listen to voices from the margins instead of falling prey to that which is easy—allowing the white, colonial heteronormative gaze to reconstruct and interpret the lives of queers on the border. However, as of late, the white, patriarchal homonormative gaze must be interpreted as a colonial gaze. On homonormativity, see Lisa Duggan *The Twilight of Equality? Neoliberalism, Cultural Politics, and the Attack on Democracy* (Boston: Beacon, 2003). Also refer to Linda Heidenreich, "Reflections on Euro-Homo Normativity: Gay and Lesbian Studies and the Creation of a Universal Homosexual," *Critica* (Spring, 1999): 41-49.

[102] *El Paso Times,* May 1, 2002. Lovie Gilot reported the story.

[103] *El Paso Times*, March 4, 1998. The story by Laura Smitherman also shows that in 1997, one-third of the anti-gay hate crimes occurred on a school or college campus, a twenty-two percent rise over the previous year, which was attributed to crimes reported to LAMBA.

[104] I am referring to Walter Benjamin's "historical emergencies" of national and global consequence" that Eng, Halberstam and Muñoz refer to in their essay, "What's Queer About Queer Studies Now?", 1.

[105] Lionel Cantú Jr., "DE AMBIENTE: Queer Tourism and the Shifting Boundaries of Mexican Male Sexualities, " *GLQ* 8, nos. 1-2 (2002): 144-145. Cantú cites the study by James R. Curtis and Daniel D. Arreola to point out how these zones of tolerance were created in

Mexican border towns in the early twentieth century so that deviance and profits could be controlled. "Male homosexual and transvestite bars" on the Mexican side of the border became the *zonas,* the "legitimized spaces for 'immoral' activity that attracted sexual tourism from north of the border." James R. Curtis and Daniel D. Arreola, *"Zonas de Tolerancia* on the Northern Mexico Border," *Geographical Review* 81 (1991): 333-47. Also refer to Cantú's recent publication, *The Sexuality of Migration: Border Crossings and Mexican Immigrant Men* (New York: NYU Press, 2009) for a more detailed analysis. The anthology, *Queer Migrations: Sexuality, U.S. Citizenship and Border Crossings* (Minneapolis: University of Minnesota, 2005), edited by Eithne Luibheid and Lionel Cantú Jr. is also a superb collection of essays.

[106]Manuel Madrid, Feb. 23, 2002, 1.

[107]Armando, July 4, 2002, 11. He did not give his last name.

[108]Yolanda Leyva, August 31, 2001.

[109]Refer to Sarah Schulman, *Ties that Bind: Familial Homophobia and Its Consequences* (New York: New Press, 2009). Schulman introduces a razor-sharp critique of familial homophobia while offering excellent examples of how lesbians use patriarchal laws against each other, particularly in child custody battles.

[110]Jorge García, December 5, 2021, 1-5.

[111]Pepe Porras, August 22, 2001, 1, 20, 23.

[112]Porras, 4. For an early discussion of "passive" versus "active" sex for gay men, see Tomás Almaguer, "Chicano Men: A Cartography of Homosexual Identity and Behavior," *The Lesbian and Gay Studies Reader,* ed. Henry Abelove, Michèle Aina Barale, David M. Halperin (New York: Routledge, 1993) 255-73.

[113]David Andrew Rubalcava, November 29, 2000, 1, 5, 8-15.

[114] José Muñoz, *Disidentifications: Queers of Color and the Performance of Politics* (Minneapolis: University of Minnesota, 1999). I am drawn to Muñoz's critique of prominent queer theorists and how he notes what Chela Sandoval refers to as "the apartheid of theoretical domains." In other words, for too long, theorists have operated in separate but unequal academic discussions. Hegemonic or first world theorists read each other's work, cite each other's work and are transformed by each other's work, while US third world theorists read

hegemonic first world theorists, cite first world theorists at the same time that we read, keep up with and are transformed by US third world theorists. Unfortunately, there is not enough exchange between and among cultural critics and theorists and the same dynamic has begun among queer theorists. If indeed, as queer theorists we are all, for the most part, concerned with what Foucault refers to in the *History of Sexuality* as power and its relation to the constructions of knowledge, then perhaps as queer theorists it's time we listen to each other more. Hiram Pérez, in his essay, "You Can Have My Brown Body and Eat it, Too!" *Social Text* 84-85, nos. 3-4 (2005): 188, addresses the manner in which queer theory has become invested in protecting "white, patriarchal, structures of knowledge."

[115] Myrna Avalos, December 5, 2021, 30-1.

[116] Gloria Anzaldúa, *Borderlands/La Frontera: The New Mestiza* (San Francisco: Aunt Lute Books, 1987), 216. From the poem, "To Live in the Borderlands Means You."

[117] Macarena Gómez-Barris, in *The Extractive Zone*, offers a vivid assessment of extractive capitalism in specific regions of contemporary Latin America (Ecuador, Bolivia, Chile) in which the "thefts, borrowings, and forced removals" of "resources from Indigenous and Afro-descendent territories" are actively rejected by "female, gender-nonconforming, working class, and 'cuir' populations" (2017, xvii). Gómez-Barris's study complicates the decolonial by turning to "perspectives," which, for me, are linked to the imaginary.

[118] I cannot speak with any authority or expertise about Indigenous feminists' works on the decolonial, although I do acknowledge the extensive writing and interventions that have compelled us as scholars to consider settler colonialism seriously. I appreciate and refer to the works of Joanne Barker (2018), for example.

[119] Jacques Lacan (2007) defined "real" and "imaginary" as a kind of cyclical journey that reinscribes the real with the imaginary again and again through the symbolic. There's no escaping how the imaginary creates the real that will become the symbolic real for many, not unlike notions of "nationalism," so that burning a nation's flag becomes an act of "real" terrorism.

[120] When I refer to "brown" imaginaries, I am borrowing from José Esteban Muñoz (2009) and his conceptualizing of brown as affect and category to describe brown queers who feel our way through and

about a world that often despises brown and queer. I would also posit
that Juana María Rodríguez (2014) dares us to desire differently as we
imagine "sexual futures and queer gestures" within Latina longings.

[121] We are witnessing the dangerous ascension of white supremacy in
Trump's "America" that sanctions xenophobes who call the police
to report black men and women because "whiteness" is "threatened,"
that rips brown children from the arms of their parents to place them
in cages, that screams to brown and black people to "go home" as if
they are not "citizens." We are witnessing that which is the historical foundation of this insular nation: racism.

[122] I'm aware that discussing "experience" is much too "touchy-feely"
for most academic, rational, Western-trained minds. I'm asking that
we acknowledge the phenomenology of experience, not only as critique, but also as transformative and activist. Referring again to Joan
Scott's (1988) "experience" is still useful; I also believe that Nelson
Maldonado-Torres is leading us down that path as he ponders the
experience of "being."

[123] *The Chicana Motherwork Anthology* (Caballero et al. 2019) offers
an analysis and hopeful critique of the way in which Chicana mothers have always relied on a community for holistic healing alterna-
tives within collective actions. I believe we need more writings from
women of color moms, queer of color moms, and transmoms of
color raising our children in incredibly difficult times.

[124] What of German jurist Karl Binding's "life unworthy of being lived,"
attributed to those who "have neither the will to live nor the will to
die"? In "Life That Does Not Deserve to Live," a chapter in Homo
Sacer: Sovereign Power and Bare Life, Giorgio Agamben (1998,
136–43) cites Binding's "pamphlet in favor of euthanasia," published
in Germany in 1920. Agamben posits that the pamphlet urged the
question of sovereignty over one's will to live or die vis-à-vis the
"value" or "non-value" of life. I'm also interested in asking: when
the biopolitics of race and gender are considered, how is the will to
live or die decided, and by whom, since white racialized bodies are
deemed more valuable?

[125] In *The Universal Machine*, Moten cites Levinas and questions the
phenomenology of "individuating" that emerges from the usual suspects—Nietzsche, Husserl, etc. It is as if the "universalizing" of personal experience dismisses the "the soloist" who "refuses to be one

and this consent not to be single worries the joint composure of phenomenology, ontology, and politics past the point of distraction, where the lineaments of an aesthetic sociology await their incalculable arrangements. This swarm is on the way, and wants to help make the way to that rendezvous, happily consenting to such diffusion while counting on you to push it along" (Moten 2018, x). I'm fascinated by Moten's phenomenology because he is pointing us toward the communal aspects of a concept that has relied too much on the soloist as alone instead of always already part of a collective.

[126]In the film *Frida*, with Salma Hayek, we see the tragic accident that debilitated her body and learn how she coped with disability for the rest of her life. As she is initially recuperating at home, bedridden and struggling with extreme physical pain, her college boyfriend, played by Diego Luna, brings her a stack of books to read. One of the books is a philosophy tract by Schopenhauer, and as he hands her the book, he says, "Schopenhauer, because it's good for you." For decades that comment riddled me, and finally after thinking about "will" in its many forms and my own impulse to theorize and actualize our understanding of the will to feel, it hit me. Frida's boyfriend wanted her to begin to feel a will to live again.

[127]Sara Ahmed's *Willful Subjects* (2014) continues to inform how I am ruminating about the will to feel.

[128]I've been reading Hegel again to scrutinize his metaphysics as dialectic. I'm asking about the spirit, the psyche—how can we possibly acknowledge what remains "unseen" to the mind, which wants to see affect on the body? How do we measure affect? We don't. We can't. An idealist of sorts, Hegel offered a three-pronged dialectic—thesis, antithesis, synthesis—that was in the realm of metaphysics, not Marxist materialism, and hence was dismissed or negated as "not real," as if ideas do not create the real, as if language does not construct realities.

[129]See Maurice Merleau-Ponty, The Primacy of Perception (1964), especially chap. 5 "Eye and Mind," pages 159–90, in which the philosopher states his initial ideas on the "visible and invisible." I suppose in my own way I'm attempting to name the psyche as invisible, beyond the flesh, which is visible even in its affect, which can be "felt."

[130]I do want to address colonial genders and colonial sex at some point.

For now, I will say that most scholarship falls into a trap of the "conquest" metaphor, set within a historical moment, to explain that which may have already existed. To assume that there is some kind of pure gender or pure sex before conquest can smack of essentialism and historical erasure. At this point, I would argue for more historical specificity to garner information on various experiences of gender and sex.

[131]We deserve to be angry when white supremacists massacre brown and black people and immigrants and indigenous people and Muslims and queers and transwomen and transmen. When this nation's government and the racist leader of the white supremacists condones racial hatred, we deserve to be angry.

[132]Rodríguez gestures toward the freeing up of our affective bodies so we may constitute new sexual futures, an incredibly freeing will to feel.

Acknowledgements

Thank you to friends, the scholar/activists who linger here continuing to inspire me: Adela Licona, Alicia Gaspar de Alba, Alma López, Angela Crow, Antonia Castañeda, Arturo Madrid, Bernadine Hernández, Catriona Rueda Esquibel, Deb Vargas, Deena González, Francisco Galarte, Jamie Lee, John Márquez, John Michael Rivera, Juana María Rodríguez, Keta Miranda, Luz Calvo, Lydia Otero, Marta López-Garza, Maylei Blackwell, Michelle Telles, Natsu Saito, Scarlet Bowen, Thomas Kinney, Ellie Hernández, Ernesto Chávez, Estevan Rael Galvez, Aida Hurtado, Alex Stern and Ward Churchill. Gracias to Adela for her stunning photograph and to Cara Hagan, artist in the photograph. To friends who help ground me: Evy Valencia, Evangeline Mendoza and Britta Van Dun. I'm forever grateful to my resilient parents Emma Zepeda Pérez and José Camposano Pérez, to my irrepressible sisters, Sonja, Cris, Yolanda, and to my kind-hearted brother J.R.

Many thanks to Arte Público Press: Nicolás Kanellos, Gabriela Ventura Baeza, Marina Tristán and staff who facilitated the publication of this collection. I'm fortunate to be housed at The Southwest Studies Center and to teach for Gender/Women's Studies at the University of Arizona. Colleagues, students and staff are kinder than I could have imagined.

I have tremendous gratitude for the upcoming generation of scholars, queer/trans and BIPOC who push ahead, advocating for new ways of being in the world. I'm pleased that some of my early words and concepts have assisted in some way. I look forward to the newness you bring. We need you.